SABAH
UNDER THE RISING SUN
GOVERNMENT

SABAH
UNDER THE RISING SUN
GOVERNMENT

Stephen R. Evans

Opus Publications
Kota Kinabalu
2007

iv

Published by

Opus Publications Sdn. Bhd. (183100-X)
A913, 9th Floor, Wisma Merdeka Phase 1
P.O. Box 15566
88864 Kota Kinabalu, Sabah, Malaysia
Tel: 088-233098 Fax: 088-240768
e-mail: info@nhpborneo.com

Sabah: Under The Rising Sun Government
by Stephen R. Evans

ISBN 978-983-3987-24-5

First privately published 1990 by the authors
Reprinted 1999
This edition published 2007 by Opus Publications Sdn. Bhd., Kota Kinabalu

Printed in Malaysia

Contents

Preface

Forty-nine years ago today (1941-1990), thousands of families in the United States, USSR, Poland, France, Britain, Burma, India, Indonesia, Malaysia, Philippines, China, Korea and many other countries continue to mourn for their relatives and friends, and in Japan victims of the atomic bombs (August 6 and 9 of 1945) which killed or crippled 447,000 people in Hiroshima and Nagasaki excluding those who were to suffer later from exposure to gamma rays, still die of terrible agony each year.

A Japanese newspaper describes the horrifying experience of the effect of atomic bombs as follows: –

"Suddenly a glaring whitish pinkish light appeared in the sky accompanied by an unnatural tremor which was followed almost immediately by a wave of suffocating heat and a wind which swept away everything in its path.

Within seconds thousands of people in the streets and the gardens in the centre of the town were scorched by a wave of scaring heat. Thousands of people were killed instantly others lay writhing on the ground screaming in agony from the unbearable pain of their burns.

Everything standing upright in the way of the blast – walls, houses, factories, and other buildings – was annihilated and the debris was spunaround in a whirlwind and was carried up into the air. Trams were picked up and tossed aside as though they had neither weight nor solidity. Trains wereflung off the rails as though they were toys. Horses, dogs, and cattle suffered the same fate as human beings. Every living things was petrified in an attitude of indescribable suffering. Even the vegetation did not escape undamaged. Trees went up in flames, the rice plants lost their greenness,the grass burned on the ground like dry straw.

Beyond the zone of utter death in which nothing remained alive, houses collapsed in a whirl of beams, bricks and girders. Approximately three miles from the centre of the explosion, lightly-built houses were flattened asthough they had been built of cardboard. Those who were inside their houses were either killed or wounded. Those who managed to extricate themselves by some miracles found themselves surrounded by a ring of fire. And the few who succeeded in making their way to safety died twenty or thirty days later from the delayed effects of the deadly gamma-rays.

Some of the reinforced concrete or stone buildings remained standing, but their interiors were completely gutted as a result of the blast.

About half an hour after the explosion, whilst the sky all around was still cloudless, a fire rain began to fall on the town and continued for about five minutes. It was caused by the sudden rise of over-heated air to a great height, where it condensed and fell back as rain. Then a violent wind rose and the fires extended with terrible rapidity, because most Japanese houses were built only of timber and straw. By the evening the fire began to die down and then it went out. There was nothing left to burn. Hiroshima had vanished."

To recall the horrible experience of the Second World War, is not merely to grieve and mourn, but also to pay tribute to those who had fought courageously for the future of mankind, for the preservation of world civilisation, in a given battle against fascism and militarism.

During the Second World War, the bloodiest and most destructive in the history of mankind, over 50,000,000 people lost their lives, of whom 27,000,000 died in the battle field. Statistics revealed that sixty-one countries which accounted for eighty percent of the world's population were involved in the war.

A large share of the burden of struggle with Japanese militarism fell upon the peoples of China, Korea, Burma, Indonesia, Malaysia and the Philippines, and other East and South-East Asian countries, which waged a struggle for their freedom and independence during the Second World War. Millions of people of these countries died in the war – in combat, in prisons and concentration camps, due to illness, murders, tortures, starvation and air-raids.

Such knowledge and awareness of the bitterness and cruelty of war will help us today in the fight against the evil forces of aggression, for peace, democracy, progress and a better future for all Nations of the world.

This book is dedicated to all those who suffered and died in the hands of the Japanese Army, especially Sabahans during World War II. The value of a local hero's memory lies not only in his own personal achievement, but to an infinitely greater degree, in the inspiration of the examples he leaves behind. The deaths of thousands of Sabahans loyal to the allied cause will not be forgotten. "SABAH UNDER THE RISING SUN GOVERNMENT," may awake unhappy memories, but it was the spirit behind it which really mattered, and without that spirit the people would have signed their own death warrants under Japanese Military Rule.

Finally as always, I thank my wife, Jane, for encouraging me to write this book. This one, by its nature, was harder than usual.

Datuk Stephen R. Evans
SPDK, PGDK, JP
6th July 1990.

Acknowledgement

The author wishes to thank Sentosa Development Corporation, Singapore, for their permission to re-print the photographs at the Surrender Chambers.

And also to Mr. Rod Wong Khet Ngee for his assistance in the preparation of the manuscript and the use of his computers and to Madam Theresa Chong Chok Ken for typing the manuscript.

Grateful thanks are also due to all my friends, Dusuns/Kadazans, Chinese, Bajaus, Malays and Muruts who have kindly provided me useful information to enable me to write this book.

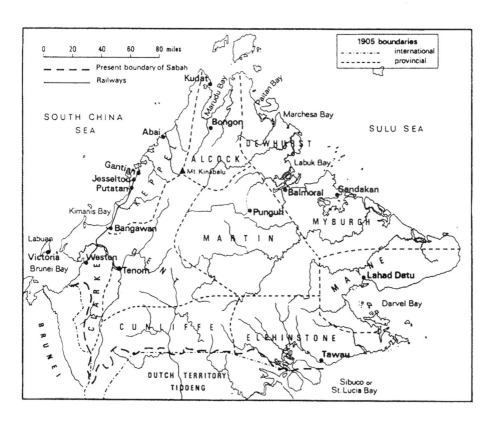

North Borneo Map – 1905

1

Early History of Sabah (British North Borneo)

Of the early history of Borneo, little is known. The Arabs knew of it as a land rich in precious stones, gold, oil and spices. The Brunei name for North Borneo is Sabah, and Saba mentioned in psalm 72 may perhaps refer to it. Kublai Khan, it is said invaded the country about 1300 A.D. Chinese settlements in Borneo existed as early as that date.

Of Europeans, the first to arrive in these waters were Spaniards. The companions of Ferdinand Magellan, after the death of their chief in the Philippines visited Brunei in 1521. Pigafetta, who accompanied them, has left a description of that town and of their voyage from Brunei to Balambangan and Banggi Islands in Kudat, Sabah, where they stayed to repair their ships.

In 1527 the Portuguese sailed along the North-West coast of Borneo and we read from early history that De Menezes on his way from Malacca to the Moluccas sailed north of Borneo and tried to enter into friendly relations with His Highness the Sultan of Brunei. From Brunei he travelled eastward.

The first Englishman to visit Sabah (North Borneo) was Captain Cowley, who visited a small island which lay near the northern end of Borneo in 1665. In 1773 the East India Company founded a trading station on the Balambangan Island, but two years later, the pirates attacked and destroyed it.

The Sultans of Brunei and Sulu exercised a nominal control over the country, while headhunters roamed the forests and pirates infested the seas. The headhunters were Dusun/Kadazan and Murut tribesmen, and of the two, the Dusuns/Kadazans were the first to give up the practice. The pirates were Illanuns, Balanini, Bajau and Suluk living in the Southern Philippines and on the coast of North Borneo. Their vessels were of large size, mostly out-triggered, measuring approximately ninety feet long and heavily armed. In Sabah (North Borneo) their strongest lairs were in Marudu Bay and Tunku Island. Rajah Brooke persuaded the Government to suppress piracy and the Sultan of Brunei ceded Labuan Island to serve as a base for anti-piracy operations. The last pirates stronghold at Tunku was destroyed in 1879.

The Sultans in those days farmed out the rights of collecting revenues to Natives of rank, such as the Pengirans or Panglimas, who engaged lesser men, the Penghulu, to serve them. Muslim law prevailed along the coast and tribal customs were respected and recognised up-country, where the people had not been converted to Islam.

The practice of farming out the revenues attracted Europeans to make a bid for this class of business. British, Americans, Germans and Austrians all competed for concessions. In the event that followed, the British won.

Sir Alfred Dent, head of an important firm in Hong Kong led the British merchants. His associates included Boron de Ovenback who was the Austrian Consul-General in Hong Kong, a man of courage and ability, Sir Rutherford Alcock, who became Chairman of their provisional association to make terms with the British Government and Mr. Richard Martin, a member of the well-known banking house of that name. The Sultans of Brunei & Sulu both responded to British urgency.

The Sultan of Brunei appointed Sir Alfred Dent to be supreme ruler, with the titles of Maharajah of Sabah (North Borneo) and Rajah of Gaya and Sandakan and the Sultan of Sulu added the titles of Datu Bandahara and Raja of Sandakan, both granting absolute power of life and death over the inhabitants. Sir Alfred Dent thus became the founder of a state, though he never ruled it, and when Mr. Gladstone, Prime Minister of a Liberal Government advised Queen Victoria to grant her Charter to the British North Borneo Company, the Company acquired the sovereign rights of Sir Alfred.

The Chartered Company was to be purely British in character. It could not transfer its territory without consent. It could trade but could not grant a general monopoly. It undertook to abolish slavery, to administer law and justice with regard to Native Laws and Customs and not to interfere with the religion of the people.

Its Governor were appointed with the approval of the Crown and several civil servants of the colonial office served in North Borneo as Governors before moving to higher posts. The list of Governors includes distinguished administrators such as Sir Hugh Clifford, Sir Ernest Birch and Lord Milverton in their young days.

William C. Cowie, who did so much for the Chartered Company, was not one of the early associates. He was a young Scotsman, a ship's engineer, who aspired to acquire lands in North Borneo as Rajah Brooke had done in Sarawak. He came out from Scotland with a few companies on a steam launch, made friends with the Sultans and established trading posts at Labuan and Sandakan. He supplied the Suluks with arms and ammunition in their fight against the Spaniards, who then ruled over the Philippines, and for a time traded in partnership with the Sultan. Many years later when the Chartered Company was securely established, he joined the Company and rose to be its Chairman. His resource and enterprise did much to advance the interests of the Company and his friendliness with the Sultan proved to be of great value.

Trouble soon arose when a younger relatives of the Sultan protested against the loss of their birthright. The most important of these was Mat Salleh, of the family of the Sultan of Sulu by marriage into it. He waged war for many years, until he met his death in Tambunan, from a machine gun bullet fired at his fort from over a mile away. Lawless tribes such as the Muruts, led by Antanom and Alisan, resisted taxation and were subdued only after fights in the distant Rundum and Tagal valleys. In spite of these events, North Borneo has been remarkably free from unrest.

Unknown regions of the Interior Residency were explored and slowly brought under control. At first the Company engaged professional explorers, such as Witti, who most unfortunately, lost his head to the Muruts headhunter in the distant Lagunan Valley and Hatton, who was accidentally shot. The task then devolved on the District Officers. Lands not included in the original concessions were acquired from time to time and together they now make up a compact country of about 29,500 square miles.

When on 1st November, 1881, the British Borneo Company received a Royal Charter to administer the territories which the Sultans and other Chieftains had ceded to these merchant ventures of London and China the administration was comparatively a simple matter. It rested on one man, the Governor of the territory.

The Chartered Company in London appointed the Governor with the approval of the Crown to govern the country. The British Government disliked the use of the title, Governor, and persisted in calling him the Principal Representative of the Company in Borneo – a phrase used in the Charter. He made his own laws by proclamation. The Governor was also chief judge so that he not only made his own laws and administered them but also interpreted them. There were of course certain safeguards, and the Crown had power to appoint inspectors to enquire into matters in North Borneo if the Crown thought fit to do so. The Chartered Company took care to appoint the best man available, and some of the most distinguished administrators in the Colonial Civil Service had served in North Borneo. The system of Government in those early days may perhaps be best described as a benevolent autocracy. The shareholders in London were satisfied to get scanty dividends by giving concessions to capitalists rather than by taxing tribesmen. They relied also on a flow of immigrants for labour on the concession.

Early history tells of a certain amount of unrest and even of rebellion at the beginning of the Chartered Company's rule, and the first balance sheets showed that the cost of fighting the rebels much exceeded the revenues. The financial position in those early days was not assisted by the protestations of fastidious and panicky auditors, who criticised the queer accounting made necessary when the Government fought tribesmen using the capital of a Company, and the capital account constantly needed replenishment.

The people of the country soon received a share in the administration and began to conduct affairs in their small townships. Sanitary Boards were set up in 1901 to look after hygiene, and though their duties were humble and unobstrusive, the members of those boards might well have labelled Privy Councillors for that is what they really were. These Boards still function after fifty years of service.

The Legislative Council first met in 1912. Sir West Rideway, a member of the Liberal Party, a former Governor of Ceylon and Chairman of the Committee which had drafted the Constitution of the Union of South Africa, was elected by the shareholders in London to be the chairman, and later President of the Chartered Company. He forthwith set out for Sabah (North Borneo). On his arrival in Sandakan (Former Capital of Sabah) he stayed at the Government House, borrowed the only motor car in the country, drove down in state and opened the Legislative Council with as much ceremony as could be achieved. He then left the Governor and members to their debates. The Council consisted of official and unofficial members nominated by the Governor with regard to representation of industry and commerce rather than of races. No Native Chiefs were appointed to the Legislative Council, because none spoke English and could not understand the proceedings. No executive was set up, and the Governor sought advice from whom he thought fit.

After the establishment of the Legislative Council, legislation by proclamation ceased, and legislations was enacted with the advice and consent of the Legislative Council. The Court of Directors of the Chartered Company in London, however retained the right to legislate for the territory and exercised this power on a few rare occasions, for instance in emergency on the outbreak of war.

A Native Advisory Council was also set up in 1914. Those Native Chiefs having authority and influence attended. Each was honoured by the title of Orang Kaya-Kaya (OKK). He has privileged to send his sons to a school instituted for the sons of Native Chiefs, in order to train the youths in the way they should go to succeed their fathers. These Chiefs gave valuable advice and the Chartered Company's Governors were careful to secure their consent to any new schemes affecting Native welfare, particularly in such matters as land, liquor, education and elementary hygiene. Native taxation was constantly under review by the Native Chief's Advisory Council.

The Chartered Company, formed by Royal Charter and not under the Company Acts had many privileges but it also had many obligations. It held sovereign power in North Borneo on the one hand, but it could be sued in English law – courts on the other. The court of Directors which administered the affairs of the Chartered Company in London kept themselves well informed about matters in North Borneo, but they interfered as little as possible with the administration in North Borneo itself.

In the year 1891 the number of people living in Sabah (North Borneo) was 67,062 as shown in the census record. Another census was made in 1931 which showed that the population of Sabah (North Borneo) had increased to 206,444 of these, 170,223 were Natives of Sabah. In 1941 the population of Sabah (North Borneo) was 300,618. During the fifty years rule of the Chartered Company, the population of Sabah (North Borneo) had increased more than four times. The reason for this was simple, because good Government had stopped piracy, tribal war, head-hunting and serious diseases, all of which had caused numerous deaths among the people. The Island of Labuan (Now Federal Territory) had a population of 8,963. Of these, 5,342 were Natives and 3,319 Chinese.

Mr. D.J. Jardine became Governor of North Borneo in 1934. Jardine's education policy was to provide more schools in Sabah (North Borneo) because there were very few schools then. A standard school building was finally introduced. Physical training was started, pupils received free dental treatment and they were given free toothbrushes. School uniforms – two pairs a year were issued free of charge throughout Government schools in Sabah (North Borneo). The number of Schools in 1941 increased to 142 with the following breakdown: – 9 Anglican, 23 Roman Catholic, 16 Borneo Basel (Protes-

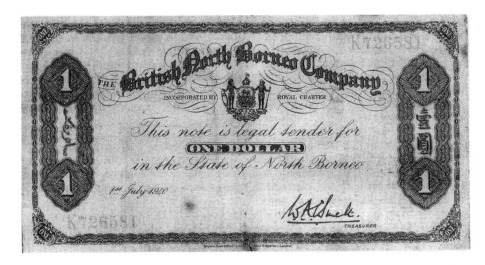

The Kinabalu Currency one dollar note used in British North Borneo (Sabah) in 1940 just before the Second World War.

The Kinabalu Currency one dollar note used in British North Borneo (Sabah) in 1930.

tant), 3 Seventh Day Adventist, 17 Chinese and 21 Government Primary (Malay). The big change here was the number of Malay medium Government Primary Schools, 21 in all, which was established as a result of Jardine's educational policy. Labuan had six schools. Three were Chinese, one Roman Catholic, one Anglican, and one Government Primary.

Government revenue was $4,045,000 and expenditure was $2,432,000. The biggest item of revenue was Customs duties and of expenditure, wages and salaries. There was only one Bank in Sandakan with a branch in Kota Kinabalu (Jesselton). The Chartered Company had its own currency (Notes & Coins). The dollar was worth the same as the Straits dollar, 2 shillings and 4 pence Sterling.

Rubber was the chief export by 1941 and valued at $14,444,000 with timber next at $2,220,000 cutch $629,000 and hemp $570,000. Tobacco exports were worth $452,000. The main imports were rice $1,452,000, cloth and clothing $810,000, food stuffs $683,000. The only European trading firm was Harrisons and Crossfield Ltd.

Hospitals were built at Labuan, Kota Kinabalu (Jesselton) Sandakan, Beaufort, Kudat, Keningau and Tawau. Cholera and smallpox had been eradicated, but malaria and tuberculosis were still classified as serious diseases. There are some leprosy cases around Putatan area and those suffering from leprosy were cared for at a settlement on Berhala Island near Sandakan. For mental patients, there was a mental hospital at Buli Sim-Sim on the outskirts of Sandakan. Roads in North Borneo (Sabah) in 1941 totalled 232 miles. Of these, 134 miles were metalled, and the rest were earth roads. There were also 600 miles of good bridle paths, over which travellers on ponies and buffaloes could move easily. The North Borneo Railways as has been seen, run daily passengers and goods services from Kota Kinabalu (Jesselton) to Beaufort and from Beaufort to Tenom and Melalap. The Weston line ran the same services, from Weston to Beaufort South. In the years between 1881 and 1941 the Chartered Company Government made great strides, but there was still much of North Borneo (Sabah) untouched, and as far as development is concerned, there remained a great deal more to be done. The end of the Chartered Company's rule came on 1st January, 1942 when the Japanese invaders arrived at Labuan, Mempakul and Beaufort. The last years of the Company's rule are covered by the governorships of D.J. Jardine & C.R. Smith. The years that followed between 1941 to 1946 were years of destruction, when almost all which had been carefully built with much difficulty, was completely destroyed, due to the Second World War.

2

Japanese Activities in Malaya and Borneo Before the Outbreak of the Pacific War

There are five kinds of Japanese Secret Agents operating in South-east Asia known as the 'Mysterious Thread', under the pretext of trading and investing, underlying Japan's principles and strategy, before the outbreak of the Second World War, of penetration by economic, espionage, and propaganda agencies prior to military action.

In practice, it attained its most complete expression in Japanese activities in Malaya and adjoining British territories. The nature of those activities by a nation nominally at peace with the territories affected has had few parallels in history. The surprise attack on Pearl Harbour and Malaya in December, 1941 was preceded by years of preparation for such an eventuality.

Japanese penetration in South-east Asia was part of a general expansion which began immediately after the Meiji Restoration in 1868. This movement was predatory from its earliest days, simply as an attempt to solve the economic problem presented by the disbanded feudal retainers or "RONIN", developed first into a three-pronged drive against Asia and Oceania and subsequently into the aggression of 1941, which was partly based on a fanatical belief in certain quarters in the possibility of world domination by Japan. In executing its policy, the Japanese Government primarily was interested in the following: –

1. Tapping and developing fuel and other natural resources bearing vitally on national defence.

2. Securing cotton, timber, and other industrial resources.

3. Dispatching colonists and emigrants.

4. Seeking a further outlet for Japanese merchandise.

5. Developing fishery and marine resources.

Other elements of spy network in controlling bodies linking Japanese trade and investment activities were the big development companies which had their ramifications in

Malaya in the form of various subsidiaries, the interests of big financial groups, such as the Nissan group and the Ishihara Sangyo Kaiun Kabushiki Kaisha (I.S.K.K.K.) the Consulate-General, the Singapore Japanese Chamber of Commerce, the Singapore Japanese Planters Association and other official and semi-official organisations.

The Nissan combine was another powerful group of industrial interests represented in Malaya, and it was of an equally undesirable character. This confine was one of the most powerful in Japan, and took over all the heavy industries in Manchuria under the name of the Manchuria Heavy Industry Development Company. It had interests in mining, trading in iron-ore, and in the fish trade in Malaya and the South Seas. It also controlled the Dungon & Gual Pariok iron mines, rubber estates in Johore and at Tawau in British North Borneo and the Borneo Fishery Company at Si Amil Island and had a working agreement with the Taichong Kongsi, a Japanese concern conspicuous in the Singapore fish trade.

The Japanese fishing fleet based in Singapore operated in an area bounded on the east by a line drawn roughly from Saigon (Vietnam) to Labuan, on the south by the Netherlands East Indies, and on the west by a line from Rangoon (Burma) to the Andaman Islands. Boats from the Si Amil Island Fishing company based in Borneo also worked in this area. The area further to the east appear to have been the preserve of boats based in Formosa (Taiwan). To the south, fish were scarce , but for shell-fishing, Japanese boats went as far as the northwest coast of Australia.

In general, the choice of area for any one particular voyage depended on the season of the year. The most profitable areas however, were the waters off the Sarawak coast, the Siam and Indo-China coasts, and the Banka Straits between Java and Sumatra.

By 1938 there were twenty-three Japanese fishing concerns in Malaya, all based in Singapore with the exception of one, the Penang Fishery Company, which operated from Penang with two power boats and three sampans. There was also an important firm, the Borneo Fishery Company, operating from Tawau in British North Borneo. This was one of the most successful Japanese fishing enterprises in the South Seas, its main output, consisting of tinned and dried bonito. The firm had a capital of one million yen, and was connected with the Mitsubishi interests. The Company had its fishing settlement on Si Amil Island, at the entrance of Darvel Bay in North Borneo where there was a Japanese population of nearly 300, and an ice factory and a canning factory served by a fishing fleet of five diesel boats, three bait boats, and two lighters.

The Nippon Sangyo Gomu K.K. was one of the largest Japanese planting concerns in British territory, being capitalized at six million yen and owning estates in Tawau in British North Borneo (Sabah), and in the Batu Pahat, Kluang, and Kota Tinggi districts of Johore, exceeding 27,000 acres in extent nearly 18,000 acres of which carried rubber trees. Later, the company extended its planted area by absorbing small Japanese rubber estates in various parts of Johore. In 1935, it took over the Washio Rubber Estate, and the Suzuki and Matsumura estates near Batu Pahat. In 1937, it absorbed the Hayami Rubber Estate of over a thousand acres in the Kota Tinggi district, on the death of the owner, Taro Hayami. The company decided in August 1937 to increase its capital to ten million Yen, and in 1939 this was further increased to 15 million Yen.

The object of the increased capitalization was stated to be the expansion of hemp production and the commencement of veneer manufacture, but it was probably also necessitated by the need for development of its acquisition in Johore and the lease of an additional 5,875 acres of land at Tawau (Sabah) making its total holding in Borneo more than 27,000 acres.

The control of the Nippon Sangyo Gomu K.K. by the Nissan group, and the fact of the latter's close connection with the Japanese army, would naturally lead one to suspect that the estates of the Nippon Sangyo Gomu K.K. might be the centre of secret military activities in addition to rubber growing alone. An example of the kind of activity undertaken by some Japanese rubber planters was provided by the visit of Kiyohiko Samejima to Singapore, in November 1937. Samejima was an assistant of the Tawau Rubber Estate of the Nippon Sangyo Gomu K.K. in Borneo. He arrived in Singapore from Sandakan on 9th November visited the Japanese Consul-General at least twice, and left again for Tawau, by way of Java on the 19th November, 1937. He had been carrying out investigations in the Interior of North Borneo (Sabah) and went to Singapore to report the results of his researches. It was reliably learned that while in Singapore, he was known to have remarked to a relative that he was returning to North Borneo to carry on his work as a secret agent, possibly assuming the identity of a Chinese servant for this purpose. Samejima operated from Tawau district, where there were nearly 700 hundred Japanese residents, at the time of his visit to Singapore, fifty percent of the Japanese were fishermen, with most of the rest engaged in the rubber, coconut, and hemp estates around Tawau. These would have been willing sources of information for Samejima and other secret agents.

Contact with Japan was maintained by a Japanese steamer which called regularly at the Tawau (Sabah) settlement.

One of the most clear-cut examples of participation by a rubber company in the intelligence activities of the Japanese community overseas was to be found in the records of Nomura and Company. This firm for some years had a head office in Bandjermasin (Southern Borneo), a branch office in Singapore, and estates in Northern Borneo and Sumatra. An interesting feature of the concern was its sudden expansion after August, 1940, when Japanese intelligence activities entered their most aggressive phase following the fall of France to the German invasion. The firm then opened new offices in Bangkok, at Sungai Golok on the frontier between Siam (Thailand) and the Malay State of Kelantan, and in Hainan Island, off the China coast.

It had under consideration plan to open an office in Batavia (Indonesia) and to open up a rubber estate near Sandakan in British North Borneo. These were main facts which made it reasonable from the intelligence point of view to assume that the sudden expansion of Nomura and Company was connected with the coincidental expansion of Japanese intelligence activities. In the first instance, the company had long been suspected by the Dutch and the Chinese of being an intelligence agency. Secondly in January, 1941, the manager of the strategically situated Sungei Golok office was arrested by Thai authorities for making a map of the surrounding country and Police buildings. Finally,the address of the firm's office in Hainan was c/o the Naval Intelligence officer.

During the same period, the Japanese were found to be taking a great interest in British North Borneo (Sabah). In October 1940, Taniguchi, the Japanese Consul at Sandakan (East Coast Residency and pre-war Capital of Sabah), made a general tour of British North Borneo, Brunei, and Sarawak, all of which were in his consular district, undisguisedly selecting suitable landing places for an invading force.

Subsequently, a number of 'diplomatic couriers' arrived from Japan in rapid succession, and in February 1941, the Consul sent T. Suzuki of Kuala Belait, Brunei, to report to him in Sandakan. Apparently Taniguchi was rather nervous while carrying on these intelligence activities for he complained that security officers were closely watching his movements, and had connection in his office and house. Following these complaints of surveillance, and lively official exchanges about the size of the consular staff which Japan proposed to maintain at Sandakan, Taniguchi was transferred to Siam (Thailand). He was replaced by Kiichiro Yamoto.

The mushroom growth of these and other bodies, both semi-official and unofficial, interested in the extension of Japan's influence to the south, and tightening control over them exercised by the Japanese Government, represented the final phase of the advance to the South which preceded the outbreak of war in the Pacific. In this respect, it became clear that the Japanese were not merely extending and intensifying their activities in the south on a hitherto unprecedented scale, but were mobilizing and strengthening the system of expansionist organisations, so that Japan would have all the necessary machinery ready-made and at its disposal to commence total exploitation of the areas concerned after the advance to the South had reached the climax of armed invasion.

While the Japanese army and navy were laying their plans and making their dispositions for the attack on 7th December, 1941 the undercover fifth-column system to assist them and the machinery of exploitation to follow in their wake, were being perfected. Japanese commercial aggression concentration in Malaya and Borneo was part of the expansionist movement, a movement primarily political, and had as its final aim, not merely successful competition in the trades and industry of Malaya and Borneo, but ultimately complete military and political control of the British territories.

3

Japanese Military Ideology and its Objective

Japan's aggressive tendencies had shown the world much earlier, when without warning, Japan attacked China in 1895 and Russia in the Far East in 1904. The victories contributed to the notion that Nippon could and should expand her territory and influence to other parts of Asia and the Pacific.

With limited land and natural resources and expanding population, Japan had no alternative but to look beyond her territory to find solutions in solving her problems.

Under the aegis of the Greater East Asia Co-Prosperity Sphere, Japan expanded her interests in the Pacific, preaching anti-colonialist sentiment by advocating 'ASIA FOR THE ASIANS'. Japan was also strengthening her army and navy.

In 1931 Japan invaded Manchuria in China and set up a puppet Government. Although Japan had signed a Naval treaty with the United States in 1922, which limited the size of the British, American and Japanese navies, Japan renounced the agreement in 1936 and built up her navy until it is at par with those of the British and the American.

Historically, the United States had officially been committed to maintaining China's independence, and when the Japanese troops in Manchuria invaded the main land of China in July, 1937, armed conflict between the U.S.A. and Japan began.

In Europe, Germany and Italy were paralleling Japan's aggressiveness. The United States was increasingly torn between conflicting nations, because the impulse towards her isolationist traditions, and on the other hand, United States' desire to assist friendly nations who were being threatened and swallowed by the aggressors.

On 25th November, 1936, Germany and Japan signed their Anti-Comintern Pact, and were later joined by Italy in 1937. In 1940 Japan signed a treaty of alliance with Germany and Italy which assured each country mutual assistance in time of war and set up spheres of influence for each country.

The world finally went to war in September, 1939. With the fall of France in 1940, Japan occupied part of French Indo-China and eyed the rich natural resources of Thailand, Malaya, Borneo, Philippines and Indonesia.

As Japan continued to press its militarisms policies, diplomatic relationship between United States and Japan rapidly deteriorated. In July, 1940 the President of the United States invoked the Export Control Act, prohibiting the export of strategic minerals and equipment and the flow of oil and steel and scrap iron to Japan, but when the oil embargo was imposed, Japan had a reserve of more than 6,000,000 tons of oil which could last for four years if properly and economically utilised.

In October, 1941 the conservative members in the Japanese Government, including Premier Konoye, were forced to resign. The hawkish army faction gained complete control and appointed General Hideki Tojo as the new Premier of Japan.

Meanwhile, the United States in the early 1940 was also gearing up for war, and in August 1940, the National Guard was mustered into Federal service. In September 50 U.S. built destroyers were despatched to United Kingdom and in the same month, the first peace time conscription law was enacted. In March 1941, the Land Lease Act was signed into law, making the United States for all intents and purposes a belligerent without having declared war. All Japanese, German and Italian assets in the United States were frozen in June and July. About the same time, Land Lease was extended to Russia in June after she was attacked by Germany. In August 1941 meeting between President Roosevelt of the United States and Prime Minister of Britain, Sir Winston Churchill produced the Atlantic Charter, which stated the aims of the two countries as regards to future world order.

On 3rd September 1941 the United States Government asked Japan to accept the following four principles as a basis for discussions: –

1. Respect for the territorial integrity and sovereignty of all nations;

2. Non-interference in the internal affairs of other Nations;

3. Equality of opportunity in trade and economic matters, and

4. Status quo throughout the Pacific area.

In October, the United States requested that Japan withdraws from China and Indo-China. Japan had not the slightest intention of bowing to these American demands, because it has already been planning a surprise attack on Pearl Harbour, Hawaii but Japan continued to take part in diplomatic negotiations with America. Special Ambassador Saburo Kurusu joined Kichisoburo Nomura, the Japanese Ambassador in Washington, D.C. to take part in the increasingly strained negotiations with the United States. They presented what would become Japan's final set of proposals on November 20th 1941.

The U.S. Secretary of State, Cordell Hull, countered on 26th November with proposals that he knew would not be accepted. They called for Japan to withdraw from all the conquered and occupied territories by military or diplomatic means. While the Secretary of State's proposals were being studied in Tokyo, the Japanese fleet – Akagi, Koga, Soryu, Zuikaku, Hiryu and Shokaku were streaming towards Hawaii.

The last days of November and the first week of December, 1941 were very critical to both sides. On November 30th General Tojo rejected the final American proposals and on 2nd December, the United States intercepted an encoded Japanese message directing all diplomats and consular posts to destroy codes and ciphers and to burn all confidential and secret materials.

The consulate in Honolulu, Hawaii was ordered to continue to send reports of any ship movements at Pearl Harbour, a task it has been performing in secrecy for some time. The three Winds messages announcing its military intentions, were broadcasted to Japanese diplomates throughout the World. One of these – East Wind Rain – was the code phrase for war with the United States.

On Sunday the 7th December, 1941 the two Japanese Ambassadors in Washington D.C. were supposed to present a note to the Secretary of State, at 1300 hrs Washington time, stating that the negotiations were broken off and that a State of war existed between Japan and the United States. In compliance with International Rules of War, the message was to be delivered about one half hour before the Japanese bombing of Pearl Harbour operation – TORA, TORA,TORA, but due to technical difficulties at the Japanese embassy, the note was not delivered in time until after hostilities had begun. The two Japanese Ambassadors had not been informed of Japan's surprise attack plans in advance. During the recent months the United States Government had been beefing up her Armed Forces strength and defences in Hawaii, because they knew that they were not in a proper state of readiness to meet any surprise attack. In addition to this the Army and the Navy were not under a unified command, coordination and cooperation were minimal. And the worst part of it is that, despite several "War Warnings" from Washington D.C. issued to the Pacific Fleet as early as 27th November, 1941 there is every evidence that U.S. officials did not give the Hawaii Commanders all the available intelligence about a Japanese attack planned for sometime in December, possibly in Hawaii. Joseph Grew, the American Ambassador in Tokyo, had been advised by the Peruvian Ambassador to Japan of a possible Japanese attack on Hawaii, Joseph Grew, simply dismissed the information as another rumor, in any event, he thought he could keep hostilities from breaking out by keeping his ties with the moderates in the Japanese Government. Grew was completely wrong in his assessment.

The Pearl Harbour attack was not an isolated incident, but part of an overall plan for the conquest of South-east Asia and the promotion of what the Japanese called the Greater East Asia Co-Prosperity Sphere. The objective is to have a free hand in establishing their control over the Dutch East Indies (Indonesia), Malaya, Thailand, the Philippines, Borneo, Singapore, Hong Kong, and the islands of the southern and western Pacific. To achieve this objective, the Japanese would have to neutralize the United States Fleet in the Pacific. Admiral Isoroku Yamamoto who is a firm believer in the value of naval aircraft in modern warfare is convinced that a surprise aerial attack on Pearl Harbour, Hawaii, was the best way to keep the American fleet from interfering with Japanese Military plans in South-east Asia.

The Japanese were very impressed with the success of the 24 planes British air-raid in which three Italian battleships were sunk at Taranto, with the loss of only two aircrafts, in 1940. Such a raid by large carrier strike force on a battled-up United States fleet at

Pearl Harbour, in the minds of the Japanese, would indeed promised a similar results. Some Japanese military planners wanted to concentrate all their naval strength in Southeast Asia, instead of taking a claw at Hawaii, but their plan was rejected in favour of Yamamoto's plan. Once the plan had been tentatively approved and worked out successfully on the war-game board, the best carrier pilots of the Japanese Navy were brought together for training. They were not informed what the mission or target was. Absolute secrecy was needed, for political and military reasons. Conceivably, the differences between the United States and Japanese Governments might be settled within hours before the scheduled attack thereby cancelling it. However, if there was to be a war, the Japanese will ensure that their first blow will be a devastating surprise to the United States.

The military operation was finally approved by Tokyo in September and the following month the merchant ship Taiyo Maru sailed across the Pacific on the anticipated strike force route to make full and complete navigational observations and gather intelligence. It was happy to report that it sighted no other shipping whatsoever, during its mission. In the meantime, the Japanese consulate in Honolulu, Hawaii, continued to supply Tokyo with up-to-date intelligence report about the US military on Oahu.

As the fleet was secretly assembling in the remote Tankan Bay of the Kurile Islands, the Japanese made a sneaky point of showing that business between the United States and Japan was normal and was going on as usual. On the 2nd of December, 1941 while the attack force was well on its way, a merchant ship, the Tatsuta Maru, was dispatched for San Francisco as proof of the continuing friendly relations between the two countries. But the ship had secret orders to turn around and sail back to Japan on the night of 7th December 1941. A powerful task force was assembled to ensure that Japanese attack was successful. Six carriers namely – AKAGI, KOGA, SORYU, ZUIKAKU, HIRYU, and SHOKAKU transported more than 350 war planes. The screening unit consisted of one light cruiser and nine destroyers. Two battleships and two heavy cruisers, which constituted the support force, and three I class submarines – the patrol unit. Eight oil tankers accompanied the force to the point of refuelling.

An additional 27 submarines, including five midget submarines of the Special Submarine Attack Unit carried orders to support the main body and to inflict damage on U.S. warships. The task force was the strongest fleet ever to be assembled in the Pacific.

The Japanese fleet commander selected a motherly course, because this is quite a distance away from the normal shipping lanes. The force would sail to a point within 200 miles of Oahu's northern coast and launch its planes on 7th December 1941. To attack and destroy the American fleet early on Sunday morning – a time considered most suitable for a surprise attack, the fleet would have to be at its launching point at dawn. It was a big military gamble, sailing too close to the American fighters and bomber bases, which would surely have aircraft patrolling the seas. The risk was necessary because of the short range and limited fuel capacity of the carrier planes.

On November 26th the strike force of the Japanese Imperial Navy began its long journey from Tankan Bay. A thousand miles, North of Hawaii, on December 3rd, the tankers

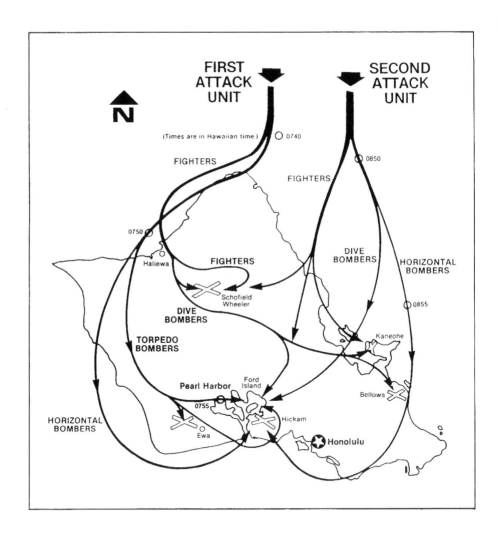

Deployment of Japanese Aircraft over Oahu

refuelled the force and sailed home. Other ships had carried drums of fuel to supply the fleet for the long round trip, to make the launching point on time.

The secret signal which Admiral Nagumo had been expecting, was successfully transmitted and received which read – "Climb Mount Niitaka" which meant that all diplomatic efforts between Japan and the United States had failed and the order was to proceed with the attack. Just after daybreak on Sunday, 7th December, 1941 (8th December 1941 in Japan) float planes from the cruisers flew over to Pearl Harbour and Lahaina to make sure that the fleet was indeed at Pearl Harbour.

At 6.00 a.m. the first carrier aircraft was launched on their flight into World War II history. The Pearl Harbour attack devastated the Pacific Fleet and left U.S. Pacific defences in shambles. 18 ships – 300,000 tons worth were either sunk or damaged and most of the Oahu based Army and Navy aircraft were destroyed or badly damaged. The Japanese also sunk or damaged five of the eight Pacific Fleet battleships, thus wiping out the main striking force of the United States Navy. Only one aircraft carriers escaped unscathed. The base installations at Pearl Harbour including the massive oil storage tanks also escape undestroyed, because Admiral Nagumo unwisely disregards the advice of his staff to send in a third attack. The Americans are, therefore, left with their base intact and the nucleus of a more modern fleet still in being. Two waves of attacks were sent in, Commander Fuchida leads the first strike with 40 torpedo bombers (with special shallow running torpedoes), 51 dive bombers, 50 high-level bombers and 43 fighters. The second wave is of similar total strength but with extra dive bombers replacing the torpedo aircraft.

The first strike on Pearl Harbour :

Hawaiian Time : 07.55
7th December 1941
(Sunday)

Washington D.C. Time: 12.55
7th December 1941
(Sunday)

London Time: 17.55
7th December 1941
(Sunday)

By 9.45 a.m. the raid was over. Most of the pilots got back to the carriers between 10.30 a.m. and 1.30 p.m. Twenty nine of their Comrade in-arms were shot down over Oahu or crashed into the sea. In the game of war, it was a small price to pay for the devastation inflicted on American ships and aircraft. Just before noon on Monday 8th December, 1941, President Roosevelt addressed a joint session of Congress and made his famous "Day of Infamy" speech calling for a declaration of war. Within days, the United States had declared war on all Axis powers – Japan, Germany and Italy.

In line with United States Politics, on 7th January, 1942 President Roosevelt submits the budget for 1943 to U.S. Congress. The total of the appropriations is US$59,000,000,000 (US$59 billion). Production in 1942 is to be 60,000 planes 45,000 tanks and 8,000,000 tons of shipping, in 1943, 125,000 planes, 75,000 tanks and 11,000,000 tons of shipping.

Pearl Harbour was not the sole target of Japanese military exercise on Sunday, 7th December 1941. While Vice Admiral Nagumo's Vals, Kates and Zekes were still airborne, Japanese bombers and fighters were taking off from airfields in Formosa (Taiwan) to attack selected targets on Luzon in the first phase of a plan drawn by the Japanese Imperial officers to give them control of Luzon Island in fifty days and of the entire Philippines in three months. To their north-west, nine infantry battalions supported by ample artillery and six squadrons of aircraft – 20,000 men altogether – moved south towards the lightly held British Colony of Hong Kong, and west of Luzon. In the Gulf of Siam a convoy of 22 ships was closing up to the coasts of Thailand and Malaya (West Malaysia) to put ashore an army which in five months would clean sweep all British power, from Singapore to the borders of India.

Malaya (West Malaysia) and Burma were the main Japanese objectives of gigantic military and naval planning and movements of the closing months of 1941. Those land plus the islands of the Dutch East Indies (Indonesia), would provide spoils to allow Japan to continue, and perhaps complete, her conquest of China, begun in 1937, and also to realize her long-term strategic aspirations of driving Europeans away from the Far East and establishing Japanese Empire in their place. Malaya produced 38% of the world's rubber and 58% of its tin; from Burma and the Dutch East Indies (Indonesia) would come all the essential oil to fuel Japan's ships, aircraft and army transport, with American naval and military bases in the Pacific either destroyed or in Japanese possessions, their movements throughout the vast area would be unhindered. Only Hitler's ambition matched that of the Japanese Imperial staff.

Honolulu Star-Bulletin – Extra dated 7th December 1941

1941 War Extra – American Newspapers

Author and wife visited Pearl Harbour on 6th November 1988

War Cemetery at Honolulu, Hawaii

Arizona War Memorial at Pearl Harbour, Hawaii

The Gallant Men who died on USS Arizona on 7th December 1941

The anti-aircraft guns used during the attack on Pearl Harbour, against the enemy, on 7th Dec 1941

The sunken battleships – USS Arizona under 85ft of water, at Pearl Harbour, Honolulu, Hawaii, still visible today (taken on 17-6-1988).

A group photo of "B" Company, British North Borneo Voluntary Force in Sanda-kan, taken before the Japanese occupation in North Borneo (Sabah) in 1939.

Standing from (Left to Right)

1 Lance Corporal Ko Yong Sing
2 Private Chan Wai Yuan
3 Private Tan Thien Kai
4 Corporal Wong Wee Man
5 Private Lim Thai Chi
6 Private Lo Kwock Chuan,
  a machine gunman in the Lewis Gun
  Section. There are only two Lewis machine gun in the "B" company.

Note: Mr Lo Kwock Chuan, now Datuk Lo Kwock Chuan, PGDK, operates a print-ing business at Kota Kinabalu, Sabah.

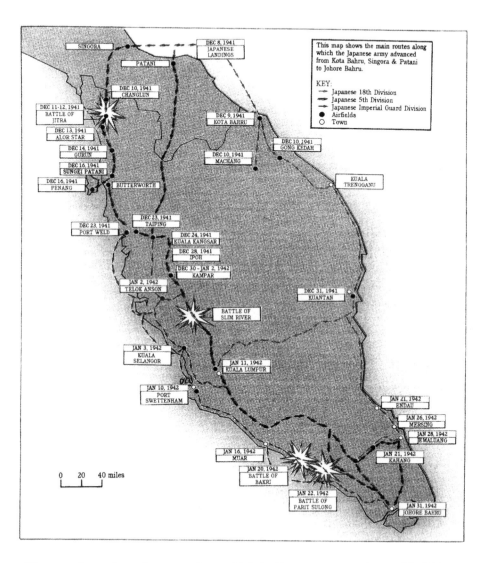

The map shows the main routes along which the Japanese army advanced in Malaya
(West Malaysia).

4

The Coming of the Invading Forces of Japan

Sabah was invaded by the Japanese Army on the 1st January 1942. Although Britain was bound to assist and defend Sabah (North Borneo) against its enemies, she found it quite an impossible task to do so, because troops and various military equipment were not available. The tragic sinking of two British Warships HMS Repulse and HMS Prince of Wales, off the coast of Malaya (West Malaysia) a few days later altered the plans for the defence of Sabah (North Borneo). The North Borneo Government was ordered not to fight against the invading Japanese soldiers. The people of Sabah was also advised to keep out of trouble with the Japanese as far as possible, for their own safety and interest and to obey orders of their new Imperial masters.

There were only two local forces in Sabah (North Borneo) at that time who could have fought the invading Japanese Army, one was the North Borneo Armed Constabulary (NBAC) who has been trained to fight, and the other, the North Borneo Volunteers (Part-time soldiers who served the then North Borneo Government without pay), had also been given some military training. The N.B.A.C. were ordered not to fight and the Volunteers were immediately disbanded.

After invading Labuan on the 1st January, the Japanese invaded the mainland of North Borneo (Sabah) on 2nd January by way of Mempakul, and on 3rd January they took Beaufort. At 9.00 p.m. (Sabah Time) on that day Lieutenant Koyama with a platoon of infantry occupied the town. They immediately made contact with their spies, collaborators and friends, particularly those who were half-Japanese, and soon they secured the services of all those Japanese citizens who had been interned in the camp at Membakut.

Doubts as to the proper duties of the North Borneo Chartered Company's officials in this emergency. The duties of the civil population in territory occupied by the enemy are set out at length in the chapter entitled – The laws of usages of war on land in the Manual of Military Law. Whether government or local officials should remain voluntarily at their respective posts and whether the enemy in occupation should continue them in their posts, if they consent to remain, will depend on their particular functions and other circumstances. As a matter of procedure, these officials will receive instructions from their Government as to the right course of action to be pursued.

On this occasion the Government at Sandakan (The seat of the former capital of Sabah, North Borneo) did not issue any instructions as to the course of action to be pursued

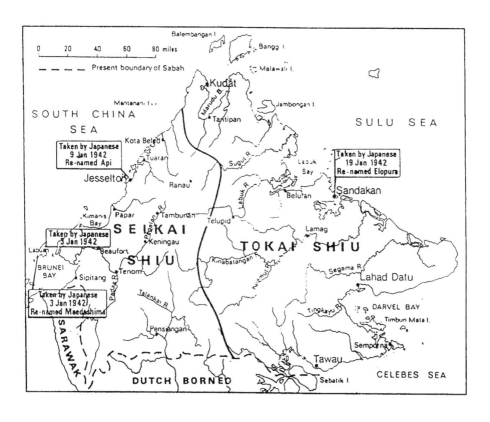

Sabah under the Japanese

by its officials on the West Coast. There was no road linking Jesselton, (West Coast) with Sandakan (East Coast) sea communication by coasting steamers had been withdrawn and radio stations were all silent. The secretariat at Sandakan was extremely busy preparing instructions for the West Coast officials in the event of surprise Japanese invasion, but they were rather slow and not ready. If the Japanese had come two days later, the Chartered Company's officials would have had their orders, but as the case is, in time of war, the unexpected always happened. The Japanese arrived earlier than was expected and they came in by the back door at Weston instead of the front door at Kota Kinabalu (Jesselton).

In the absence of specific instructions from the Governor of North Borneo, the Resident of the West Coast, and the Commander of the North Borneo Armed Constabulary met the Japanese on their arrival at Beaufort. These two officials were seriously questioned as to the state of affairs and were ordered to proceed to Brunei State under escort to meet the Japanese Commanding Officer there. At Brunei the two officials were examined separately.

The two officials were disturbed all night and then interrogated the following morning for twenty-four hours. Most of the questions put to them concerned the destruction of Japanese property in the territory of the public utility services and the breaking up of installations and property to deny their use by the Japanese. The willingness of the Chartered Company's officials in the West Coast Residency to carry out their duties under the Japanese Military Government, was also discussed in length.

The Japanese interpreter was very efficient and the parties concerned understood each other, without difficulty. The Japanese eventually decided that the Resident must carry on the administration and that the Commandant must be responsible for the maintenance of order. Both of the officials agreed to this, and they returned to Kota Kinabalu (Jesselton).

Meanwhile the Japanese had arrived in Kota Kinabalu (Jesselton) on 9th January, and they later published a document which according to the Japanese, the two officials had signed. Several copies of the documents in Japanese script have survived, but they are not all the same in every respect. A translation of a copy of the documents dated 13th January, 1942 read as follows: –

"The Resident and the Commandant have agreed to the terms and conditions of His Excellency the Commander-in-Chief of His Majesty the Emperor of Japan to continue their public duty.

The soldiers of His Majesty the Emperor of Japan will be quartered in Kota Kinabalu (Jesselton) Beaufort and other places.

The Japanese army may request supplies. The local Japanese Commander will represent the Commander-in-Chief for the purpose of control.

Important Government affairs must first be discussed with the Japanese Commander.

The British in Singapore surrendered to the Japanese, under the Command of Lt. General Tomoyuki Yamashita (The Tiger Of Malaya) on 15th February, 1942

The Japanese Commander approves that the dignity of the civil servants be upheld.

Local Police will continue to maintain Law & Order but all Arms and Ammunition must be put under the full control of the Japanese Commander.

Laws of the former Government will be enforced, but any law directed against the Japanese Government will be revoked.

Japanese people and settlers must be protected. The new Japanese currency will be of equal value to the existing North Borneo Currency and no action whatsoever, to lower its value will be allowed.

Planting, Business, Communications; Culture, Education and Religion must be restored with immediate effect.

Local produce must be sold to the Japanese, when required at a reasonable price.

All anti-Japanese activities must ceased. If there is no anti-Japanese Government activities, the Japanese authorities will protect the lives and property of all Europeans.

If these terms & conditions are carried out faithfully and to the entire satisfaction of the Japanese authority, the authority will permit the administration to continue as before."

The translation is the general statement of the terms and conditions agreed upon, rather than an accurate recital of them. As expressed, these terms and conditions appeared to be quite fair and reasonable. Each official could refuse his assistance to the Japanese Government, but each seems to have thought that he would best-fulfil his moral duties to the people of the country if he remained on duty in the presence of the Japanese.

The Japanese, at the beginning, carried out these terms and also the terms of the Hague Convention to which they subscribe, because they were signatories. The European officials on the West Coast Residency continued their services from January until the 16th May, 1942 when they were all finally arrested and interned.

The Japanese reached Sandakan, the capital of North Borneo on 19th January, and there, the Governor issued orders to the European officials to take no part in the Japanese Administration except in certain cases involving medical and staff matters. The Japanese immediately arrested and interned all the Europeans in Sandakan except the Doctors, the Electric engineer and a couple of adventurous people who went far a field and lay low for several months.

The attitude of the Chartered Company's official against the Asian in the past have not been good, however, normal relationship between Europeans and Asians in North Borneo appeared to be quite satisfactory. It is quite normal for the Chartered Company's officials to feel more superior than their Asian counterparts because they are the Government of the day who rules the Asian in the State of North Borneo. Other European rulers who rules Asian countries in various part of Asia feels the same way, and may have adopted the same attitude of being superior.

The Europeans could do little in the presence of Asian Conquerors and by prolonging their stay they distracted and unknowingly embroiled the every person whom they sought to serve. The Asian staff soon learned not to recognise and respect any European out of office for fear of being beaten or tortured by Japanese soldiers for showing friendship to the Europeans. Asian has her own salvation to work out to an ever increasing extent, and European civilians could do little or nothing to assist during war time. It was a matter for the Armed Forces.

The Constrained state of affairs on the West Coast Residency could not continue for long. After four months, the Europeans received notice to meet at the Jesselton Hotel at 0900 hrs the next morning. It was 16th May 1942. They were told to attend a lecture. The leading Asians stood on one side and the Europeans on the other.

The Japanese Commander announced that by Order of the Emperor, the Europeans were to be interned and the Asians would supersede them. The Europeans were then sent away in motor buses and taxis to collect their belongings and to lock up their houses. They were given two hours to do this. On their return to the hotel with light luggage only, they must surrender the keys of their houses to the Japanese Commander who promised to safeguard the property. The European women, most of whom had returned from up-country, were interned at St. Francis Convent and the men in the Police Barracks at Batu Tiga, until arrangements were made to transfer them all to the huge internment camps at Kuching, Sarawak.

The Japanese divided the territory (Residencies) into two Governorates. The West Coast with the Interior Residencies and Kudat was called Seikai Shiu. The East Coast Residency was called Tokai Shiu. Labuan was re-named Maedashima, the Island of Maeda, after Marquis Maeda, the Commander-in-Chief. Not long after he was killed in an air crash, the Japanese renamed Labuan Island after him and put up a stone to his memory. Kota Kinabalu (Jesselton) was named Api and Sandakan Elopura.

The Japanese also altered the calendar to fit their own into what they called "Super Space Age". Their era antedates ours by 660 years in advance, so that their 2601 corresponds to our Western Calendar 1941. Their 2602 became our 1942 and so on. 'Showa 16' is the sixteenth year of the Emperor Hirohito's reign and corresponds to our 1941. "Showa 17" to our 1942 and so on. The months and days are the same in both calendars.

The hatred of the people of Sabah (North Borneo) towards the Japanese showed itself right from the beginning and after the internment of the British officials. The attitude was increasingly hostile for various reasons. The molestation and raping of women, the conscription of women as prostitutes, the regimentation of the people of Sabah (North Borneo) to increase food supplies and to labour for their new masters, the enforced homage to the Japanese Empire and cruelty were some of the main factors. The beatings of the people and the torture in the prisons have left memories that will never fade.

No person was safe from the Japanese police. Many were beaten to death with heavy wooden and thick bamboo sticks in the prisons by cruel Japanese police and its agents who assisted the Japanese in punishing the victims. Every Japanese from the lowest ranking soldier had to be called "Tuan" (meaning, Sir). If a Sabahan met a Japanese anywhere, even in the street, he had to bow or salute the Japanese. If he did not bow or salute the Japanese, the Japanese would slap him on his face as hard and as often as he could. The culprit was expected to stand patiently while his assailant slapped him with full force of his outstretched arm and hand. The Japanese normally began gently just to warm up, but soon each blow, left/right, would eventually knock the culprit sideways, and at each blow he was expected to stand up straight and ready for the next blow. People who offended the new masters were given severe punishments without trial. These included torture and death.

As time went on life became much more difficult for the people of Sabah. The Japanese took more and more of the crops for their own consumption. People who disobeyed them were badly beaten or made to stand in the open sun and suffer severe exposure to the fierce rays of the sun, or kept in prison without trial. Taxes were heavy – even the people living in the remote areas of the Interior had to pay taxes and fines had to be paid too, for the smallest offence. The Chinese were asked to pay for more taxes because of re-mitting money home to China to assist the war against the Japanese. Sandakan Chinese had to pay $400,000 and Kota Kinabalu (Jesselton) Chinese $600,000.

One of the notices put out by the Japanese Government read as follows: –

"The Chinese must always remember that the Japanese Commander holds power of life and death over them, at the word of the Japanese Commander, they can be killed instantly".

Another most unpopular feature of the Japanese rule was the requisition of food. This accounted nominally in the case of rice for Japanese requirements to about 40% of the crops. In addition the agents and middleman made profits so that the total requisition was usually over 50% and in many cases it rose to 80%. The Dusun/Kadazan farmers, like most farmers all over the world, knew how to hide their cattle and much of their farm produce in time of war. The Natives hide their padi between false partitions in the house. Most of the walls of the houses in the Interior Residency are made of bamboo or bark and therefore adaptable for this purpose. Some hid their padi in special storage trunks made of bark and hidden in the thickest of the jungle. Hiding places were often betrayed by local spies and once the stores of food were discovered, the farmers suffered fines, imprisonment and severe beating.

The Japanese did not issue any instructions to their soldiers to prevent the molestation of women. Sabah (North Borneo) women had no protection whatsoever.

The attitude of the Chartered Company's Asian civil Servant was generally correct. There were quite a few exceptions and some of the Indian members of the service were caught up in the act of the Indian Independence League and publicly rejected their adherence to the British. In general, the Asian Public Servants earned high praise for their loyalty to the allies and for the service which they rendered during the occupation.

The Native Chiefs and Village Headmen had the most difficult task, for the reason that they had the responsibility of adjusting the requisitions of the Japanese to the resources of the inhabitants of the villages. Most of the people felt that they had grievances of this account, but it would have been surprising if there were none. As far as record is concerned, no Village Headman had abused his position to enrich himself. This had so far been proven. Traders on the other hand took every advantage of the times to enrich themselves, but the village headman, who had a position of trust and responsibility lived up to it.

The North Borneo Volunteer Force consisted of two companies, one on the West Coast and the other on the East Coast. Their training is strictly infantry. Captain Byron commanded the Company at Kota Kinabalu (Jesselton) and his subalterns were Lieutenants V.H. Benthan, J.C. Bryant and Li Tet Phui. During the outbreak of war in December, 1941 the small force was mobilised. They helped to guard the ports and landing beaches and occupied the Japanese fish canning factory at Banggi Island.

The volunteers had always hoped to have a go at the Japanese and the decision to make no attempt at defence was a disappointing experience to them. When the Japanese planes were circling in the sky above Kota Kinabalu (Jesselton) before the arrival of the soldiers and were dropping pamphlets, the North Borneo Volunteers were still under orders to remain at their posts and not to fire a shot without expressed orders. After the entry of the Japanese the Volunteers patrolled the townships without arms to maintain order for a few days, and finally returned their arms to the armoury store on 5th January, 1942.

It was to the West Coast Company that leaders of the subsequent revolt looked for men with some military training, and these men never had any doubt about their ultimate fate if they fall into the hands of the Japanese. Their willingness to resist lived on during the enemy occupation and this led many to join the Kinabalu guerrillas. In the minds of the Japanese, the volunteers are most likely to cause troubles and should there be any trouble, the source would be definitely caused by the volunteers. All the volunteers were black listed by the Japanese and their movements were carefully watched. Imprisonment or death at the hands of the Kempeitai was the price many Sabahans paid for their service as volunteers. The British Officers were imprisoned, but the Asian Officers and other ranks had to live under the iron heel of the Japanese. They stayed with their European officers to the end.

The North Borneo Volunteers deserved every respect for what they have done to their country, because they have suffered years of oblivion. Seven years later after the historical event of World War II then they received a late recognition of their services and all members mobilised during the period 10th December, 1941 to 19th January 1942 or their representatives, were finally granted three months pay and allowances. Due honour has not been paid to the survivors of these companies. They include Dusuns/Kadazans, Muruts, Eurasians, Chinese, Indians, Europeans, and other natives of Sabah. Six of the North Borneo Volunteers were executed by the Japanese. The remaining few of the old volunteers are still alive and living in Sabah.

Before the outbreak of the revolt, the Japanese had an inkling of the restless condition of the people and they knew that members of the North Borneo Volunteer force consisted of capable and resolute men with experience of the country and good leadership quality.

Each of them was called up to submit himself to enquiry partly to satisfy the Japanese as to his good faith and partly to predict his attitude towards the conscriptions of three thousand men whom the Japanese wished to recruit for military service. This enquiry helped to precipitate the open revolt because the leaders thought that their underground movements could not be kept a secret much longer. In the face of these enquiries, the leaders, including the volunteers, continued to throw dust in the eyes of the Japanese and prepared their plans for the Revolt of the Double Tenth.

When Albert Kwok led his revolt against the Japanese, he looked to the Volunteers to become comrades-in-arms in the adventure and did not look in vain. The initial success of the Kinabalu Guerrillas at Kota Kinabalu (Jesselton) owed much of their training to Lieutenant Li Tet Phui, Sergeant Jules P. Stephens (Father of Sabah's former Chief Minister, the late Tun Fuad Stephens and Tan Sri Ben Stephens, former Managing Director of Sabah Foundation) and others in the volunteers who joined in the first fight.

Some of them were very young men who hardly knew what life means, but there were older men as well who had wives and children who fully understood the danger and what the consequences would be. Very few may have endowed a guerrilla life with a glamour of their own imagining. These few would be adventurers but most of the volunteers knew that there would be much battling but no looting. They also realised that it was their duty to resist the enemy whenever an opportunity arise. To stand aside was to shirk their responsibility of defending fellow countrymen from being forced into service with the Japanese. In this they were largely successful. They rendered the young men and women of their time, a great service and they remained true to their ideals.

The Japanese pushed forward their co-prosperity plan for what it was worth, but all their efforts to influence the people of Sabah (North Borneo) to participate actively in favour of the scheme failed, because the people were paid less than half the value of the crops or merchandise they produced. Furthermore, the worthlessness of the Japanese paper currency was soon obvious to all. The Japanese currency had a printed design of bananas on the face of the notes. It is known to the people of Sabah (North Borneo), as "Duit Pisang", or banana currency, and became an object of ridicule.

The Dusuns/Kadazans, the Muruts and other inland tribes showed that apathetic frame of mind was to be expected. A great deal of loyalty was shown by the Natives, especially by those who had been in closer contact with those who had ruled them, but action was not to be expected. In the minds of the Natives patriotism is rather a love of their own part of the country, but not of the whole of it for they are only dimly aware of its size. They love the area or the district which is their homeland, and whoever, as ruler, allows them to live there receives immediate recognition. It need only be said that these inland tribes showed a customary subservience and obeyed the commands of the ruling power whoever it might be. Their warlike spirit was not quickened until others had set the example.

The Japanese kept a close control over the Native Villages through the headmen (Ketua Kampong). Spies were planted in the villages to ensure that the Headman did his duty properly.

There was no difficulty in persuading young men, after a term in Japanese prison to enter Japanese service as spies and to report on their neighbours activities. These youngsters

The ten dollars Japanese currency notes used in British North Borneo (Sabah) during the Japanese occupation/war.

The one hundred dollars Japanese currency notes used in British North Borneo (Sabah) during the Japanese occupation/war.
The people called these currency notes Duit-Pisang (Banana Money) and has no legal tender.

were well known to the villagers, but they could not be harmed without serious retribution.

Village Chiefs received from the Japanese an official badge. These badges were issued only to those who professed friendships with the Japanese and there were a few candidates. Probably the sense of security whilst wearing these badges was the real inducement. The Native like to wear a badge and takes great pride of his letter of authority "Surat Kuasa". The Japanese is aware of this, and the practice of issuing badges was one of their few administrative successes. They imitated the practice of the Chartered Company's Government. The Japanese badges which superseded the old badges, were made of tin but is attractive enough in the eyes of the Native. The badge is rather large and it looks very much like a bicycle license plate used in Sabah (North Borneo) during the colony days. The points projected awkwardly on the breast of the wearer and a large safety pin is needed to hold it in position.

There are two types of badges issued by the Japanese. One of these was a five pointed star of poor metal quality, no better than tin plate, painted with red in the centre. The other was slightly better which was made of metal, and in terms of workmanship for award to the higher ranking chiefs. The senior badge boasted an eagle with outspread wings ready to fly on the point of the star. Only three chiefs were considered by the Japanese to be worthy of wearing this emblem. The three were Chaw Ah Quee, Hassan & Musa.

The headmen were summoned to attend meetings from time to time. The object of this meeting was to persuade the village Headmen to co-operate, but the main purpose is to commit them to do whatever the Japanese required them to do without question. The Headmen had no choice but to express promises of a full co-operation and loyalty to the Japanese as their new rulers. The Japanese also demanded full information concerning the situation of each village, its productive capacity, the number of people living in each houses, their principal occupations, etc. All these details were recorded in writing. At the end of the meeting each Headmen was paid one Yen as expenses to cover his meeting attendance.

The Japanese were extremely demanding in their methods of collecting supplies. In the office in Kuala Penyu, which was standing after the re-capture of that village, there was found posted up a list of Native Chiefs, and Village Headmen, covering the area from Kota Kinabalu (Jesselton) to Beaufort. The list gave the names, the villages, and the monthly payment of each. The names included many Headmen who had served the Chartered Company's Government and who had continued to serve under the Japanese. There were approximately 60 names on the list and the monthly payments varied from $3.00 to $10.00. In Japanese currency these sums were of very small value. The highest paid Chief was OKK Yahya with $10/– per month. He carried out his task to the best of his ability in order to protect his people against Japanese oppression and of adjusting Japanese demands to local resources as well as could be expected.

There was no interference with the people's religion and customs. The small village schools in some instances continued to function, but there were no dispensaries for those requiring medical treatment, and there were no drugs or medicine available.

The former Hospital Assistants were willing to serve and remained in their respective stations, but there was no proper work for them to do due to the shortage of medical supplies of all kinds. The hospital lacked bedding, disinfectants, medicines, soap and surgical instruments. The patient's diet simply did not exist.

The village shops remained open but goods were scarce. Everything valuable had been buried for safe keeping and there were no imports worth mentioning of. Barter trading of local produces and delivery of requisitioned materials were the only activities in the townships.

The Japanese spread propaganda by telling the people that Japanese officials mixed freely with the people far more than British officials, who seldom see the people except their own officials, but this did not earn any respect for the Japanese. They insisted to be addressed as Tuan (Sir). The people became so accustomed in calling the Japanese Tuan (Sir) that it finally became permanent habit, and whenever the returning British officials asked for information, the people still referred to the Japanese as Tuan (Sir).

The British on the other hand were also called Tuan (Sir). The Japanese ideologies which had often been advertised, that they were the saviors of oppressed Asian found no response or support from the people of Sabah (North Borneo).

The people in the Interior Residency were left alone for quite sometime, but orders for supplies were soon pressed, and the Japanese then learned of the advantages of the Interior as a source of important military strategics. The Japanese then set up strong Army posts in the Interior to control the local people. Ranau, Keningau, Tenom, Beaufort and Pensiangan had garrisons. The strongest were at Ranau and Pensiangan. There were troops also in all the main coastal towns.

The Village Headmen soon found that much unpleasant duty had to be performed in collecting large gangs of labourers to improve existing roads and to construct airstrips at Kota Kinabalu (Jesselton), Keningau, Ranau, Bingkor, (which is now utilised for wet padi cultivation – called Alab Pintas Padi Scheme, Bingkor) Kudat, Sandakan and Labuan. In order to have more labourers to work in the various airstrips, the Japanese enforced "Forced Labour System".

At Sandakan about 5,000 Australian and other prisoners of war carried the burden for most of the work. At Kota Kinabalu (Jesselton) the people was conscripted for the purpose and all Government servants regardless of their race, except for the Japanese, had to work on the airfields twice a week.

In Keningau, Government Servants including the Towkays have to work on the airfields and road everyday, for at least one hour before going to their office and again for another one hour after office hours, before they were allowed to go home. This is deemed as very important by the Japanese because they wanted the construction of the Keningau and Bingkor Airfields, the bridge at Liawan River and the 14 miles Keningau to Apin Apin road to be completed urgently. During the process of the construction, more than 400 Indonesians, mostly Javanese who were brought to Keningau by way of Kuching, Sarawak, as labourers, died of Malaria, Dysentery, Beri-Beri, and other form of malnutrition due to lack of food and medicine. The work had to be carried out 100% by manpower because there was no earth moving machinery available.

The pressure imposed by the Japanese for collection of foodstuff and the enforcement of "Forced Labour" had repercussions throughout Sabah (North Borneo). In general the Dusuns/Kadazans stayed where they were, and watched with disgust Japanese soldiers shooting their buffaloes, cows, pigs, and goats and cutting down their coconut trees which they could not climb. The Dusuns/Kadazans reduced their rice harvest to a bare minimum hardly sufficient for themselves. They turned their cattle loose for fear of being taken away by Japanese soldiers, without payment.

The Chinese left the main Towns, sought shelter in their own lands and went into farming. The Muruts retreated further into the jungle and lived on tapioca, sago, and Addut, a kind of wild yam or potato found in the forest. This particular species of wild yam is very poisonous, and could be eaten only if all its poisonous juices have been extracted or trodden out of it.

The Muruts could not hunt wild animals, because the Japanese had taken all their guns. This made farming in the remote areas more difficult than ever before, because the wild animals had greatly increased in numbers and naturally caused lots of damage to their crops. The Japanese did not kill the Muruts, but they took away whatever property they had, and forced them to work in unaccustomed ways and in different districts.

At Kota Kinabalu (Jesselton) the All Saints Church, which stands on a hill site near Karamunsing, was made into a Telecommunication Station. It was a convenient site and most useful for communication system. The rectory closeby was used as a prostitution centre of the Japanese Army. It had large floor space and the area was divided into various apartments. Every living Sabahans knew of its existence unmistakenly as a Brothel House. Another brothel was set up at the Basel Mission Church and school buildings at Ridge Road and another one at Harrington Road exclusively for Senior Japanese officers. Kota Kinabalu (Jesselton) was well supplied with girls mostly Indonesians (Javanese) brought in all the way from Indonesia, (Dutch East Indies) by way of Kuching, Sarawak.

The Roman Catholic Church at Kota Kinabalu (Jesselton) served a variety of purposes from time to time. The Saint Francis Convent was converted into a Hotel for Japanese officers and one of the other buildings nearby was used as a Court House.

The Old Governor's House, near the new Sabah State museum was reserved for use by the Japanese Commanding officer and his staff, and the old Residency at Jalan Istana, was occupied by the Civil Governor, known as Gunsarikan Khaka.

The Japanese Military Police known as Kempeitai, who did more damage than good because of their cruelty, which earned them contempt and hatred everywhere, and in the following paragraphs describing police methods readers are urged to differentiate between the various police forces, which were formed from time to time. At least five groups of men must be differentiated. These were the North Borneo Armed Constabulary, the Japanese Kempeitai, The Civil Police raised by the Japanese, The Jikidan and the Police Agents – Spies.

Less than 25% of the North Borneo Armed Constabulary were incorporated into the Japanese police groups and with that proportion less than half served in the Kota Kinabalu (Jesselton) district. It is positively shown that the majority in the police force are Japanese. Every large organisation has a few black sheep, those in the Constabulary are well known to the Sabahans. The proportion of men who were imprisoned or executed by the Japanese for their loyalty to the British or who have been decorated for their courage is quite high in comparison with other Asian police forces. There are very few cases or charges of brutality against members of the Constabulary. On the other hand there are many men in the force whom the force should rightly be proud of.

Most of the cruelty and torture was inflicted by the Japanese. Native police recruited by the Japanese were unwilling spectators for the most part and offenders such as the prison warder of Labuan, nicknamed King Kong, were indeed rare.

In Kota Kinabalu (Jesselton) the police under Japanese Organisation and Control, occupied three stations. These were the Civil Police Station in South Road, the Jesselton Sports Club building and Victoria Barracks at Batu Tiga. The Sports Club building became the headquarters of the Kempeitai, and it was in this historical building and at Batu Tiga where most of the atrocities happened.

At the entrance to the Sports Club building two large wooden posts were erected as a sign of Japanese occupation and the building was split into cells and heavily furnished with barbwire windows, whipping posts and chains.

Horrible cries were heard issuing from this building throughout the Japanese occupation and many people died there from severe torture. It was in the Sports Club building that many prisoners received a fore-taste of the torture which was to follow at Batu Tiga. Here many people went through the first stages which led to removal to Batu Tiga where the final stages of torment and execution were carried out.

The lightest form of punishment was to provide sport for the crazy Japanese police. To a tree at the corner of the football field near the Sports Club, two of the alleged culprits would be fastened with a sufficient length of rope. These unfortunates had to challenge each other to a bout of fist fights. Any one who fell over at once received a beating with a stick to encourage him to renew the fight. The one who was adjudged the loser received a severe beating.

At the back passage of the Sports Club building, the Japanese police set up all kinds of ill-treatment facilities intended to force the victim to incriminate himself and others. At first the Japanese would beat the victim with a thick stick about three feet long, renewing the beatings every hour. Sometimes the victims were tied by the hands to a chain hanging from the ceiling with their knees reaching the ground. The blows were delivered on the back, the shoulders, the arms and the head. Often the poor victim become insensible and died during the beating. If he survived the repeated beatings, the Japanese Kempeitai would apply the water torture and other torments calculated to break down the prisoner's resistance and to sap every fibre of courage left in him.

Prisoners whose hands were bound behind their backs were not freed at meal time. A bowl of rice and some salt were set on a table in front of each and he had to stoop down to eat from the bowl and lick the salt like a dog.

One Japanese officer, who was put on trial by the Military Court for murder after the armistice, said that when time was limited the water torture was applied, because it was the most effective in the shortest time, to get rid of the victims. Four Japanese wardens held the victim standing up. A dripper filled with water from the bucket was held up to the   victim's mouth and the water was poured in while the wardens pressed his throat to make him swallow. Two full buckets of water would be poured down this way. The victim would suddenly faint due to the excessive weight of water inside his stomach, and then collapsed to the ground. Here, the wardens stood and trod upon the victim's back and belly until the water was forced out of his eyes, nose, mouth and other cavities of the body.

The screams of the victims resounded through the building and lessened the will power of resistance of the others while waiting for their turn, which indeed reduced their chance of holding silence in the horrible ordeal to come.

Generally the Japanese began to question the victim early but they did not question him closely. If they could afford to wait, when they had finished with him, he would be ready to reveal everything they asked him. His life was nothing more than a mere drifting mist of burning pain. After proper preparation for questioning, the victim does not tell lies.

He has no strength left to concoct false information. He has completely lost his will power. To refuse to speak, to concoct lies or to deny, when questioned, required lots of guts and will power, but it has all been completely drained from the victim.

He merely tells what he knows. The Japanese Police knew from long experience that when men are approaching the point when their resistance will break, they will eventually cry out for someone to come and listen to their confessions.

Such an act of inhumanity is not new and even European history has revealed the dark side of its history. In China a law required that no man condemned to death for a crime may be executed until he has confessed his guilt, but the Japanese atrocities committed against our people were contrary to the law of the country, which the Japanese, as the invading and occupying power, were under International obligation to administer.

The Japanese Government had subscribed to the treaties containing this obligation and each Japanese officer who acted contrary to the law of the country was liable to be tried according to the law for his misdeeds.

The Japanese Military Police engaged a large number of people including men, women and children, to form a spy network throughout Sabah (North Borneo). The people were distributed as workforce in shops, companies, villages, ships, etc.

For instance The Usira Company, engaged in obtaining provisions for the army, kept two women agents (Akibono) who were first used as prostitutes before being trained as police agents. The Kempeitai were chiefly engaged in collecting supplies because of the urgent requirements for food which overshadowed almost all the other occupations.

The workforce were stationed all over the country to supervise labour on the roads, to reclaim land for cultivation and to collect produce.

The Natives were engaged everywhere as Police Agents and formed the bulk of the new police force. When the Japanese took over control, they employed some of the North Borneo Armed Constabulary under a Japanese officer, and recruited some Natives to swell the ranks.

A small number of Sikh police were stationed on the West Coast. Subader Dewa Singh, the most senior Asian officer of the North Borneo Armed Constabulary was dismissed by orders of the Japanese on the eve of their arrival in Kota Kinabalu (Jesselton) in January, 1942 and later became one of the leaders of the Kinabalu Guerrillas at Tuaran. Sergeant Budh Singh and Corporal Sohan Singh were executed by the Japanese after the Double Tenth, at mile 5½ near the Petagas Bridge. Sergeant Bhagat Singh was killed. Most of the other Sikhs left the force after the uprising.

In April, 1943 a dozen of police sergeants were sent to Kuching, State of Sarawak, for six months training. They were taught military Commands, police duties, local laws, and the Japanese language. On their return they were appointed Chief and assistant Chief Police officers. The Japanese had no difficulty in obtaining Native Police recruits by means of the usual inducements of pay, clothing and rations in addition to the fear of possible consequences if they refuse to comply. Threats to recruits included likelihood of retaliation on their families if they did not obey orders. The Japanese realised that the importance of the work which the police were doing on their behalf and recorded that – "It is necessary to increase the number of full-time specialist police spies, so that we have sufficient manpower to dispose in areas however remote".

In a speech given by the Chief of the Military Police in Kota Kinabalu in March, 1944 he said that the police force consisted of twenty Japanese Administrative officers, forty Japanese Police officers and approximately 1,500 local policemen. Further expansion is necessary.

The Chinese did not prove to be useful policemen as far as the Japanese was concerned. The Overseas Chinese Defence Association with its headquarters in Kota Kinabalu (Jesselton) had made every efforts to separate their people from contact with the Japanese, and their activities culminated in the Double Tenth Revolt in October, 1943. When it was over and the heavy penalties had been paid, the Chief of the Japanese Military Police made an open speech in March, 1944 and called for further expansion of the Native and Indian police. He publicly admitted that the Chinese had not proved to be useful police for their purpose.

The Japanese adopted a new system of making groups of people responsible for the behaviour of persons. This system is known in China and Indonesia (Dutch East Indies) where it had been in operation long before. The new system is known as Hoko spy system. It was in fact started by the Chinese a thousand years ago and the Japanese copied it from them. The villagers under the instruction of the village Headmen provide a roster of young men whose main duty is to keep watch and set points throughout the day and often throughout the night. Small huts were provided at selected points and communication system is maintained.

Young men were forthcoming in large numbers for this service. They were called Jikidan, and were responsible to the local village Headmen. The system can serve a useful purpose at a cheap cost, and it is also capable of expansion into a spy network system. Furthermore, the system of making the whole community responsible for the behaviour of the individuals within it and is an easy way of levying fines on the whole community for the offence of a few.

Nobody dares to be too outspoken lest he is betrayed by others anxious for the safety of the whole community. This system has many advantages from the invader's point of view. It simplifies police control and the spread of Japanese propaganda, and in addition the local administration can easily work as it provides a convenient means of recruiting Native labour and auxiliaries. In this respect, it is a clear indication to show that the Japanese are good imitators of other people's efforts.

A few cases were tried in the Japanese Courts. The sentences imposed by the Courts for offences usually were not extreme or excessive, but the ill-treatment by the Police and the torture in the prisons were so brutal and inhuman that no credit was even earned by the Court in terms of justice.

Native Village Headmen also sat as Magistrates. Punishment in a few cases was quite out of proportion to the offence and in one case worthy of mention here, a member of a Eurasian family was sentenced to three years imprisonment for giving a stick of cigarette to a prisoner.

Two Natives convicted of murder in the adjoining territory at Lawas, Sarawak, were sentenced by the Native Magistrate there to fifteen years imprisonment each and the Japanese authorities endorsed the sentence imposed by the Magistrate. When the British arrived, these two criminals remained in prison fearing reprisals from the murdered man's family if they returned to their homes in the village. The British authorities confirmed the Japanese sentence and the convicted men remained in custody to serve their sentence.

The Japanese made full use of the rivers and bridle paths in the country to move their troops and prisoners from North to the South or from the East to the West. Before the war all movements between such places as Brunei and Sandakan took place by sea, and none have so far thought of going overland. The Japanese army by force of circumstances, became the first army to move in single file across the country. The rivers are of great help to the Japanese army but the journey up-stream was slow and laborious. The river valleys were unhealthy and malaria was prevalent in them, so that there was much sickness followed by high death rates.

Any prisoners who feel sick on the long marches were shot on the spot by the rear guards, as there was no means of carrying the sick.

As the Japanese advanced slowly across the country, the Natives fled into the jungle and the hills to avoid being called for work and supplies, and to save their women from molestation. Empty villages were burned down by the Japanese for no specific reason.

Two of the main centres were Ranau in the North and Pensiangan in the South, Ranau in the North received the troops who came from Sandakan by bridle paths or by boats up the Labuk river. At Tampias, where the Labuk river ceases to be navigable the troops left the boats and marched three days overland to Ranau, here they were in touch with the West Coast bridle paths and could continue their march to Kota Kinabalu (Jesselton) about one hundred miles away. Ranau also served as the junction for any troops from the Interior who might be required to reinforce Kudat.

They would follow the West Coast bridle paths to Kota Belud and then continue North East to Langkon and Kudat. Such a journey would be approximately one hundred and fifty miles.

An alternative route from Sandakan to Kudat followed the Labuk river as far as the Tungud River and so to the Sugut and Paitan rivers. From Paitan a track was developed to Pitas to meet the bridle paths. The foot track from Ranau to Tampias was widened to take pony traffic. A bridle path which is only three feet wide will greatly assist transport and became a link in the route of the Australian death march from Sandakan to Ranau.

Kota Kinabalu (Jesselton) and Sandakan were joined up, the route being Kota Kinabalu (Jesselton), Tamparuli, Dalas, Tenompok, Ranau and Tampias, and transport went forward by the River, Labuk to Beluran and then to Sandakan.

Pensiangan in the South was the depot for the transit of all Japanese troops for Tawau and Tarakan and at times two or three thousand Japanese soldiers lay in camps there. The boat journey up the Sambakong river from the East Coast to Pensiangan was rather difficult and took two or three weeks. During dry weather there was much haulage up the rapids, and in wet weather it was also difficult to make headway against the floods.

At Pensiangan the troops were in touch with the West Coast bridle paths. A long march leads Northwards for over a hundred miles to Keningau. In wet weather this is impeded by floods, and after the surrender, when the Muruts lined the path to cut off stragglers, the route became a death march for the Japanese.

At Keningau the Japanese occupied another central position and reinforcements could be sent to Brunei, Kota Kinabalu (Jesselton) Kudat and elsewhere, as and when required.

Two airstrips were built in Keningau. Another was constructed in Ranau close to the camp where three hundred Australians were held as prisoners of war. The bridle path was widened and improved between Keningau and Apin-Apin to take motor traffic. For fourteen miles the new road runs as straight as a ruler. The Japanese boasted to the people that they are clean straight forward and sincere in running the administration of the state, citing the fourteen miles straight road as an example. An old Murut headman disagreed with what the Japanese said, stating that if it was true his people would have had few, if not, no complaints against the Japanese if the Japanese hearts were as straight as the Keningau, Apin-apin road.

These improvements were lost in a country as large and mountainous as British North Borneo. Its thirty thousand square miles remained as inaccessible as before. When Sabah achieved Independence through Malaysia in 1963, development was stepped up by the Government, and all the existing undeveloped pre-war and post-war bridle paths was reconstructed into an all-weather road suitable for all kinds of vehicles.

Mat Salleh's rebellion which occurred more than 90 years ago, gave an advance example of a successful defence system of the Interior lasting for two or three years. The Dusuns/ Kadazans are not of the warlike disposition as the Muruts. The Dusuns/Kadazans were once headhunters but were not as ferocious as their Muruts counterpart. They are excellent farmers. History has shown that the Dusun/Kadazan farmers have often been exposed and subjected to plunder. They are the farming folk and it is evident that the Japanese intended to rely on the resources of the Dusuns/Kadazans and defended the Interior of Sabah. (North Borneo).

The Allied Forces on the other hand soon made the Japanese sea routes unsafe. Experienced Japanese seamen have no match against the Americans and the British seamen. The American sea patrols controlled the coasts with the assistance of the Air Force, and the destruction of Japanese cargo ships soon caused great shortages and difficulty in shipping. Under the Japanese, the economic position of the country gradually and steadily deteriorated.

There were shortages of imports of every kind of goods due to lack of shipping and decrease in production from the manufacturing countries where the goods were imported from. Local produce is not available and non for sale. Moreover, there were no ships to take the produce away and there were no other buyers except the Japanese Government and its appointed agents. Articles and goods needed for productive purposes, such as tools, were not available. Clothes, matches, fuel and drugs were hardly obtainable due to very limited supply.

The Japanese did not only fail to supply the commercial requirements of the country, but they plundered and stripped North Borneo almost everything that was valuable including tools, machinery, metals, leather and rubber. Cattle were exported in large numbers. British currency, gold, silver, brass, iron and other type of metals had to be surrendered to the Japanese. Machinery fell into complete disuse because there were no spare parts. The few spare parts left were often adapted for use elsewhere.

The Japanese made some efforts to improve the trade. One or two agents from abroad arrived to enquire into the complaints. Again, their efforts to restore the economic structure of the villages failed.

Several attempts were also made to increase agriculture produce by growing more rice and vegetables and the local Headmen were paid with a small pay to organise and carry out the same objective at village level for more production of foodstuffs but most unfortunately it benefited only the Japanese in their requisitions for more food, but not the people in general.

Japanese spokesmen admitted that the plight of the people of Sabah (North Borneo) has grown increasingly desperate and sought to improve relations by saying that the Japanese in Sabah (North Borneo) were suffering equally with the people of the country. They appealed for co-operation saying that if the Japanese were defeated in the war, the people in North Borneo would suffer even more than they were suffering during the occupation.

On the West Coast residency the food situation was quite bad however, the situation had not dropped below the famine level. The herds of cattle, the rice fields and the vegetable gardens sufficed to keep the people from starvation and to maintain their supply quotas to the Japanese. There was sufficient supply of tapioca, sweet potatoes, and yam.

It was reported that in Miri, State of Sarawak, over three thousand Chinese and Indonesians, mostly Javanese, died as a result of starvation due to lack of food. Further reports revealed that the people who were starving in Miri had been seen dragging themselves on their bellies through the streets and since they were too weak to build their own shelters and unable to look for food, they simply died by the roadside. The Natives on the other hand will never die of starvation because they eat almost every living things in the Jungle, such as, monkeys, snakes, anteaters, porcupines, crocodiles etc. whatever they could catch, by laying traps.

The Natives who owned boats does not leave their boats in the river banks, for fear of being taken away by the Japanese. Most of the boats were hidden by the Natives. No sailing crafts could be seen on the coasts. The local fishing industry came to a complete stand still all along the coastline. Fish is not available in the market.

There are two main problems encountered, these are labour and transport and also the shortage of imported goods, thereby causing endless problems, while the needs for the Japanese must come first or given top priority.

The British Kinabalu currency was worth more than the yen, and so the dollar wages and salaries of everybody were reduced to bring them into line with the wages and salaries of the Japanese themselves who were paid in Japanese Yen.

Inflation prevailed and the Japanese currency soon became valueless. After the battle of the Coral sea in May, 1942, six months from the outbreak of war in the Far East, the Japanese yen declined further in value. A box of Japanese matches cost $10.00 in Japanese currency. Based on rough estimate the British currency had about a hundred times more purchasing power and value than the Japanese currency. The Japanese currency rapidly became utterly worthless. At the end, the worthlessness of their Banana money could be judged from the capture of five tons of it in a wrecked train when the Australians re-occupied Beaufort in June, 1945. No one took the money, because it is known to be worthless.

Clothing of value was hidden mostly by the Towkays (Chinese Merchants) who owned it. The huge earthenware jars, which is so common in the villages, were most useful for storing all kinds of goods and valuable items. These jars are found in almost every Native houses and are used for storing rice, fermenting rice wine called Tapai and in ancient time, for burial of the dead.

Their tops can easily be secured by a plate stuck with resin and they made safe receptacles when buried in the ground.

Many Natives were reduced to wearing bark. A small quantity of Native cloth was made on hand looms by the women folk.

In February, 1942, before the Japanese had occupied the territories for a month they issued orders requesting everybody to deposit in the new Banks any money in excess of $30/–. Each family could keep this small sum for current expenses. The rest must be banked. All gold and silver had to be handed in and merchants were required to give a full account of their cash resources. Rubber had to be sold to the Japanese Government at a price much below that of the cost of production. No arms and ammunition of any description were allowed to be kept by its owners.

The livestock was preserved to certain extent, and an estimated loss of one-third of the cattle was considered fair at the time of the surrender. Cattle and even ponies were used for food and were requisitioned for Japanese army supplies. Draught cattle used for ploughing in the rice fields, were protected as part of the Japanese economy, but most of the rice fields were not fully planted and on re-occupation it was found that most of the buffaloes had become so unaccustomed to the plough after a lapse of three to four years that they had to be retrained to the yoke by their owners. The Indians bitterly complained of the reduction of their herds by requisition. Their herds grazed near the towns and were easy for the Japanese to lasso. Payment by the Japanese Army was enforced, but the depreciation of the Japanese currency nullified the payments.

During 1943 many Japanese firms were established in Kota Kinabalu (Jesselton), and elsewhere with the help of the Japanese Government. The produce of the country and its trade gradually fell into Japanese hands. Padi and rice were controlled by one firm, and rubber by another. A transport company was formed and all vehicles were ordered to be delivered to the Company on requisition at a price much below their real value.

The Japanese firms began by trying to build up a good stock. They collected everything they could and paid high prices. Furniture and even picture frames were in demand. But as it was to be expected the Japanese were no match for the local businessmen when it came to bargaining. In business affairs they were often the losers. They engaged local men to be clerks and storekeepers. Some of them were appointed to be brokers as well. There were positive cases when goods were purchased and paid for by the Japanese firms and lodged in the stores. Before long these same goods were taken out by the back door and brought in again at the front door, to be paid for over and over again, the process may even have been repeated for a fourth time.

Many kinds of Postage Stamps were issued during the Japanese occupation. Stamps of the four neighbouring countries – North Borneo, Labuan, Brunei and Sarawak, were pooled under the Japanese Postal Authority and that existing stocks with and without overprints were freely used. The first stamps used were the current Chartered Company's postage stamps without overprint and the usual post mark. The current stamps in use in Japan were issued. Many other issues followed. The rarest and complete set of all the occupation sets is the complete set from 1 cent to $5/– of the pre-war Chartered

Company's issue, overprinted and in use in Kota Kinabalu (Jesselton) in October, 1942. One of the reasons for its popular demand is that this particular set of stamps suffered almost complete extinction during the air-raid at Kota Kinabalu (Jesselton) before the stamps was distributed. Professional stamps collector thinks that this set must rank as one of the rarest Japanese issues in the whole of South East Asia.

For the first few weeks of the Japanese occupation no postal services at all were available and the public knew that their letters would be liable to censorship, confiscation and delay. Although quite a number of mint on Japanese occupation issues existed, but they are very few postally used specimens.

As China was at war with Japan the position of the Chinese in Sabah (North Borneo) was indeed precarious. Few held the status of British subjects or citizens and the Chinese as a whole had supported China's war against Japan for many years. The Japanese issued a proclamation to the effect that all property belonging to the Chinese in Sabah (North Borneo) was confiscated to the Japanese Government.

The safety of their lives and the possession of their property depended solely upon the will of the Japanese High Command. They lived at the mercy of the Japanese. Their life was marred by the strain of extreme fear and uncertainty and by the continuous bullying visits of the cruel Japanese police.

Any Chinese who were known to have been leaders in the local Organisation of the China Relief Fund for carrying on the Chinese struggle and war against Japan were sought. Three were arrested, sentenced to long term imprisonment, and sent to Kuching, Sarawak, to serve their punishment there.

This act caused much hatred and being the first of its kind, it is a clear indication to show the Chinese people what they might expect later from the iron hands of the Japanese. The Japanese followed this with a demand for a public subscription to support their own war. Sabah (North Borneo) was called upon for a million dollars, six hundred thousand dollars was charged upon the West Coast and the remainder, four hundred thousand dollars, was charged upon the East Coast.

The leading Chinese merchants were very heavily assessed and any traders and land owners who could not draw money from the Banks, borrowed at heavy rates of interest to discharge their liability.

The compulsory subscription caused many land owners to borrow money from various people who had been more successful in adapting themselves to the enemy occupation and had money to spare. Seeing this as a golden opportunity to make money, the Blackmarketeers came to the fore, and those who were influential with the Japanese, truly found their opportunity.

Land owners may have very good reason to challenge some of the unfair deals during those days but nobody dare to point it out to the Japanese. A prominent Chinese businessman associated with Tay Bee Yong Brothers, died in the Hospital in January 1943, due to severe mental distress as a result of misery. The Chinese community was shocked to hear about his sudden death and strongly felt that it was a serious loss to the whole Chinese community of Sabah. (North Borneo)

To the credit of the deceased Towkay, stood the payment of $100,000.00 (one hundred thousand dollars) to the compulsory fund as the deceased Towkay's share to save the Chinese from further Japanese harassment.

Poll Tax was also enforced at the rate of six dollars per person from each male Chinese. This was collected for one year only, because of the revolt which this taxation plus other measures caused.

Entertainments and dinner parties were also offered to the Chinese merchants, who openly accepted the invitations, but despised their hosts. These invitations were failures for the purpose for which they were issued. They were designed for co-operation but soon became ominous because guests who accepted the invitations and attended the function were on certain occasion, sent to prison.

Frankly speaking, the object of the dinner party is to record every invited guests' name for the purpose of his condemnation. In spite of the obvious danger of attending this official dinner party, many could not resist the temptation offered by the Japanese for a good meal. The people were easily attracted, like ants, because those who attended the dinner party was given a kati of sugar as a present.

It was customary for the Japanese to celebrate the National days of their fellow countrymen, partly to provide a counter attraction and partly to urge the people to recognize the Japanese public holiday. To the annual dinner on 9th October, the eve of the Double Tenth, a large number of local celebrities would be invited and Japanese officers would be present. The Japanese knew that 10th October was a day on which the Chinese morale in particular would be exalted, and for the purpose of conciliation, correction or counter blast, all and everybody would be summoned. The annual public dinner on the eve of the festival was announced to be given at the Emperor's expense. The practice had many disadvantages, because it brought the leaders of the people under the eye of their masters on the eve of the very day when a disaster might be expected, it professed sympathy for the ideals of the subject people and it displayed a show of Japanese force just when it might be needed. But the Kinabalu guerrillas attacked on the eve of the Double Tenth in spite of all these precautions.

To collect guests for such a dinner, the Japanese often had recourse to the precedent set in the parable. The highways and hedges had to be searched for likely guests who could be compelled to attend and swell in numbers. Excuses for non-attendance were often given in reply to the invitations. It was risky to refuse, but more risky to accept. On these occasions the Japanese practised the inhospitable habit of announcing the latest list of proclaimed offenders, some of whom might even then be seated at the table.

The Japanese learned to respect the Dusuns/Kadazans, with whom they were in contact much more than with the Muruts. The Dusuns/Kadazans have a pleasant habit of putting all strangers and visitors to tests of skill. They have their own forms of contest and self-defence. A villager called Tumanggong Bin Kandawau, who hails from Kg. Liawan Ulu,

Keningau, told the author, how he challenged one of the Japanese officers to a fight, with any weapons he chose.

The Japanese would not trust Tumanggong, so he measured off a stick the same length as the Dusun/Kadazan Sword, and gave it to Tumanggong to fight with. The Japanese used his own sword, a Samurai, in the test of fighting skills. Tumanggong rapped the Japanese officer twice over the head smartly, before the Japanese realised whom he was up against. Tumanggong was never hit by the flat side of the Japanese sword. The Dusuns/Kadazans have their own kind of "Ken-Do" unknown to the Japanese. This game did much to engender a respect for the Dusuns/Kadazans.

The Japanese themselves often went hungry, and the troops on their long marches starved when they could not contact the local villages or lost their way. Their urgent means of survival and great appetite for meat incited them to cannibalism.

In Sabah (North Borneo) there were several cases of cannibalism. First of all there was a case involving a Dusun/Kadazan headman at Bundu Tuhan. It was reported that he had been partially eaten by a group of Japanese soldiers. His grave was eventually discovered and when it was dug and opened, the corpse showed the hacking away of pieces of his flesh.

The grave was again opened in 1946 for further investigation to prove the case of cannibalism. The second case involves two Australian prisoners of war, who escaped from the Japanese staging camp at Muanad river near Beluran, on one of the death marches. The Muanad river is approximately seven miles away from Beluran and at mile 56 the foot track approaches the bank. The two Australians made their escape down the river and were seen by the Natives. The Japanese went in pursuit and on their return, were seen carrying fresh human flesh. The Natives never saw the two Australians again. During the incident food was very scarce everywhere and there is every possibility to account that this is another case of cannibalism. There were reports that Japanese troops in the West Coast Residency were eating young Dusuns/Kadazans. Reports on cannibalism seemed quite unbelievable, but on the 17th October 1945, Orang Kaya Kaya Lajungga, the Dusun/Kadazan District Chief of Penampang, confirmed that the reports were correct.

There were also another statement of facts from the Australians themselves, who had been captured by the Japanese and survived to tell us of their horrifying experience that on one occasion, a Native and an Indian guard were killed and eaten by the Japanese. The stage between Tampias and Ranau on the death march was indeed a very difficult one to traverse, and this is well known to every travellers who has travelled on the same routes. It is mountainous all the way, and there are no villages. A good walker would be able to reach his destination within three days.

During the march, the Japanese from one of the camps selected one of the healthiest Jikidan and took him away from guard duty. The Jikidan never returned, for the simple reason that since the Japanese practised cannibalism, the poor Jikidan must have been dumped into the Japanese cooking pots.

There was another blood-chilling story about a Native who was sent out by the Japanese to hunt wild pigs or deers. His hunting trip had not been successful, so he came back empty handed. This did not please his hungry masters, and in return the poor hunter was killed and eaten by the Japanese.

A Japanese Officer attached to the transport section in New Guinea signed a confession that he had eaten the flesh of an Indian, who had been killed and cut into pieces. On 14th October, 1945 the Japanese Army Headquarters at Tokyo, Japan, admitted that it has officially approved cannibalism when food shortage occurred amongst its troops.

The Japanese troops were permitted to eat only the flesh of the enemy's dead. A death penalty will be imposed on any Japanese soldiers who ate their own dead, which was considered the worst crime in the army, as far as military history is concerned.

The English Law does not provide punishment for cannibalism, during the Second World War. It is hoped that the British Parliament had by now introduced a law against cannibalism. The Japanese soldiers could, on the other hand be punished for mutilating dead bodies under current military Law. A dead body should by right be given to the executor representatives, relatives, or family members of the deceased and in this particular case, cannibalism in the Penal Code is more or less theft of a corpse. The killing and eating of a person is definitely murder, in the eyes of the Law.

There was no records whatsoever of Chinese having been put into Japanese cooking pots. Natives and Indian police were eaten, but not the Chinese. It is presumed that they had left too bitter a taste of a different kind in the Japanese mouth, after the Double Tenth.

One militant minded Chinese openly expressed that indigestion in the Japanese stomach was a proof of the success of the Chinese revolt against the Japanese, and that this alone made it worthwhile.

The Japanese sank further to its final degradation of the monster that perish. We pray that those who took part in this evil and monstrous activities most inhumanly were comparatively few, and it is hoped that this horrifying history based on personal experience during the war, when Sabah was under the Rising Sun Government, shall never happen again.

5

The Kinabalu Guerrillas

When a country is attacked by an enemy with larger and more powerful army than its own, the best way of handling the situation would be to split its forces into small bands who act on their own, attacking and worrying the enemy, striking at them when they are not prepared, hitting them hard and running away.

This kind of war technique has been waged for many hundreds of years, but the word 'guerrilla', which means 'minor war' was first used for this sort of fighting by the Spanish who used it against the armies of Napoleon in the Peninsular War, in the year 1808 to 1814. Faced with a similar situation, the people of Sabah (North Borneo) formed the Kinabalu Guerrillas to fight against the Japanese.

In May 1941, before the war with Japan, Albert Kwok of Kuching, Sarawak, arrived in Kota Kinabalu, (Jesselton). Albert Kwok a Chinese, was born in Kuching, where his father worked as a dentist. Albert Kwok was sent to Shanghai for his education and escaped from there when the Japanese invaded the city. He travelled extensively in China, visiting Nanking, Hankow, Canton and elsewhere. He studied Chinese medicine, and was very successful in treating prevalent and distressing complaint known as piles. His practise was a large one. He treated some of the highest ranking officials in China and West Malaysia (Malaya) and he received much recognition for his curative skill and also for his zeal in the interest of China. It is said that Albert Kwok earned merit from Chiang Kai-Shak Generalissimo himself. He was sent to meet the Japanese as the invasion spread south, and was appointed to be an intelligence officer of the Chinese Government. He returned to Borneo by way of West Malaysia (Malaya) in late 1940. He was a bachelor and lived with his sister and his brother-in-law in Kota Kinabalu (Jesselton).

In appearance he looked young, of middle height and strong built. He was neat and clean shaven. He was a man of superabundant energy. He made many friends. When his stock of medicine was exhausted he gave up business. Probably every person in Kota Kinabalu, (Jesselton) and the neighbourhood knew that he was planning to overthrow the Japanese. Though there were many spies around, none has betrayed him to the Japanese. His attempt has brought him local fame, and posterity is likely to hail him as a local hero and a patriot. His mother lives in Kuching, Sarawak, and a brother and sister are attached to the Sarawak Government Service.

Kwok heard in Dutch Borneo (South Kalimantan) there was a party of Dutch, British and Americans still holding out in a place called Long Nawan. In February, 1942 he tried to make his way there through Pensiangan, but found that when he got to the Sabah (North Borneo) border it was strongly held and guarded by the Japanese. He could go no further because the rivers were carefully controlled. He therefore returned to Kota Kinabalu (Jesselton). It was wise he did so because in August, 1942 the Japanese suddenly fell upon the settlement at Long Nawan and killed everyone they found, there were - men, women, and children.

Not long after Albert Kwok's return from Pensiangan, the Japanese sent out an order. The order was dated the 13th June, 1942 and said, amongst other things, "Let not the Chinese forget that the power of seizing them and putting them all to death rests with the decision of the Japanese High Command". By "High Command" they meant the Command in Borneo, not in Tokyo, Japan. This showed Kwok that he must really do something in Sabah (North Borneo) to oppose the Japanese.

In this, it means the Second World War. Men who fought against the invaders either openly or secretly, were called resistance fighters. Albert Kwok found out that there was a resistance movement in the Republic of the Philippines.

Through a businessman in Kota Kinabalu (Jesselton) called Lim Teng Fatt, he got to know a Filipino named Imam Marajukim who was in close touch with Alejandro Suarez, the Philippines resistance or guerrilla leader. The Imam was a Muslim priest, but he was also a trader and a very fine sailor. Suarez had sent him to Sabah (North Borneo) to find out what was happening in Sabah (North Borneo). As a trader in sugar Imam Marajukim came to Lim Teng Fatt's shop where he met Kwok.

Early in 1943 Kwok and the Imam went to Sulu to visit Suarez. The guerrilla leader was not too happy about Kwok at first but soon came to trust him. Kwok learned a great deal about guerrillas warfare technique during his stay in Sulu, and when he returned to Kota Kinabalu (Jesselton) in May, 1943 he was very determined to proceed with his guerrilla movement.

He first made contact with the Overseas Chinese Defence Association in Kota Kinabalu (Jesselton) and collected $11,000 and medical supplies to assist the Sulu resistance forces. He also enrolled about two hundred men to fight. In June, 1943 he made another visit to the Republic of Philippines with Imam Marajukim, taking his cash and his medicines with him. He was then given an appointment as a Lieutenant in the United States Army by Suarez on the 1st July 1943 and sent back to Sabah (North Borneo). He reached Kota Kinabalu (Jesselton) on 10th September 1943 and started to re-organize a group of re-sistance fighters against the Japanese, as well as to help collect money for the Overseas Chinese Defence Association. Kwok could count on help from the Chinese for his secret guerrillas.

The Islanders were also keen to join and so were many of the Volunteers who had been disbanded. The Dusun/Kadazan farmers and the Muruts of the Interior were not ready for the revolt. Though they hated the Japanese, they hated still more the risk of losing their homes and having their families ill-treated. To this, there were two exceptions. Musa, the leader who had fought against the Chartered Company Government, and was at that time living at Membakut, agreed to form a guerrilla band. Musa did not have a chance to fight, but was nevertheless put into prison by the Japanese.

The other was a Murut, former Chief Inspector Duallis, who kept up resistance to the Japanese right to the very end, killing many of them in daring raids.

Albert Kwok called his small band the Kinabalu Guerrillas Defence Force and made his headquarters at Menggatal. He encouraged leaders to form groups at Inanam, Tuaran, Kota Belud, and Talipok. He also planned to form others in places South of Kota Kinabalu (Jesselton) to link up with Musa at Membakut. Hiew Syn Yong, an Assistant District Officer commanded at Kota Belud, Mr. Charles Peter, formerly Officer-in-Charge of the Police district at Kota Kinabalu (Jesselton) was at Tuaran, with Subedar Dewa Singh, another ex-policeman, Kong Sze Fui, was at Menggatal, and Mr. Jules Stephens (Father of the late Tun Fuad Stephens, former Chief Minister of Sabah, and Tan Sri Ben Stephens, former Director of Sabah Foundation) as Adjutant, was the organizing chief. Jules Stephens had been a Sergeant in the North Borneo Volunteers. The Chief of the Islanders was Panglima Ali, who was a Village Headman of Suluk Island, off Kota Kinabalu (Jesselton), with Arshad of Kg. Oudar (off the mouth of Menggatal River), Jemalul, of Mantanani Island and Saruddin of Dinawan Island.

The Kinabalu Guerrillas kept in touch with Suarez in the Philippines through Lim Teng Fatt. Lim owned a boat and was a good seaman. He was made Captain in the American Army by Lieutenant - Colonel Alejandro Suarez, commanding the 125th Infantry Regiment, then serving in the tenth military district of the United States Armed Force in the Philippines. Lim was also in contact with Major F.G.L. Chester, a British officer, serving with the Australian army, who made frequent visits to the East Coast Residency of Sabah (North Borneo). Major Chester had been a Rubber planter on the West Coast of Sabah (North Borneo) and knew the country well. Through Lim he warned Mr. Charles Peter not to start anything with the Japanese until the Allies were ready to help. He made it quite clear that no help could be given until the time is ripe.

Lieutenant Albert Kwok made rapid progress with his scheme for resistance against the Japanese and was working on expansion plans when most unexpectedly everything was changed. He learned that the Japanese were going to take 2,000 young Chinese men and forced them to join the Japanese army. These forced recruits were to form garrisons at places in the Interior Residency and on the islands and so would relief Japanese troops for other duties.

This was a blow to Chinese pride and also a serious threat to Kwok's plans for a resistance army. All the men he has counted on to assist would be taken away, and Japanese troops would be free to hit back the guerrillas in any part of Sabah. (North Borneo)

This was not the only blow. Kwok also learned that the Japanese intended to seize a large number of Chinese girls and force them into the service of Japanese army as prostitutes. They were also going to call up all the former North Borneo Volunteers for immediate military duty. To take the girls would bring great shame on hundreds of Chinese homes. To take the Volunteers away would mean the end of the guerrilla bands. Kwok made up his mind to strike.

Against him were of coercion the regular Japanese Army, the Japanese Military Police

(Kempeitai) and the local police under full Japanese control. There was also a force, the Jikidan (irregulars) who were set in villages to watch their fellow country men and report their movements. There were few regular troops stationed in Kota Kinabalu (Jesselton) and some in the coastal towns.

There were Japanese Army garrisons in the Interior, mainly concentrated at Ranau and Pensiangan. In Kota Kinabalu, there were three places where the police were stationed, these are, the Police Station in South Road, the Jesselton Sports Club, which was the headquarters of the Military Police, and the former North Borneo Armed Constabulary depot at Victoria Police Barracks, at Batu Tiga.

There were also police garrisons at Tuaran and Menggatal. Another well guarded place were the old Customs buildings inclusive of the wharf and godowns at Kota Kinabalu (Jesselton).

On Albert Kwok's side he had about one hundred of his Kinabalu Guerrillas and approximately two hundred and fifty men mostly islanders. Most of his men had no military training. Charles Peter, Dewa Singh, were ex-policeman and Li Tet Phui and Jules Stephens had some part-time experience as soldiers. The rest were new to the business. No written orders of the force have been kept. It is most likely that there were none, for security reason?

People have different views of what Kwok's plan really was. Some feel that he intended to knock out the Japanese in Kota Kinabalu (Jesselton), hold the town and rally supporters to his banner, then with the assistance of the Allied Forces throw the Japanese out of Sabah (North Borneo).

The people knew that Kwok was a man of principle who always looked into the bright side of things and hoped for the best, but they all know for sure that Kwok is no fool. It is more likely that he hoped to strike a blow at Kota Kinabalu (Jesselton), and rouse up the other resistance groups to advance their objective against the Japanese, while he pulled back hopping for help from the Allied Forces, and for the supply of Arms and provisions from Suarez of the Philippines.

With this aid he could keep up attacks against the enemy until the Allies invaded and drove the Japanese out. The other speculation is perhaps Kwok hoped only to strike a desperate blow against the Japanese, losing all in the effort but at least making the enemy think again and drop its plan to enslave the Chinese youths and girls. Nobody can really tell what Kwok really hoped for, but we do know he sent for arms and ammunitions from Suarez and planned the burning of the Kota Kinabalu (Jesselton) godowns so that the blaze would attract attention and assistance from a friendly ship or submarine from the Allied fleet.

It is also known that through Lim Teng Fatt, he had been informed that the Allies could not help and had been advised to keep quiet until a more favourable time. But as it had been seen, he has no other choice but to proceed with his plan.

The Chinese youths and girls were just about to be conscripted and the North Borneo

Volunteers had been rounded up by the Japanese and ordered that they would shortly be required to report for duty.

Albert Kwok had a very difficult decision to make, but eventually decided to strike after much deliberation. He fixed the rising against the Japanese, on the night of October 9th, 1943, the eve of the great Chinese festival of the Double Tenth.

This particular festival is to mark the success of the Chinese revolution of Dr. Sun Yat Sen. He thought that if the Sabah Chinese could celebrate the festival as free men, it would do wonders for their spirits too. Kwok's plan for the assault on Kota Kinabalu (Jesselton) was simple but required good organization and careful timing.

A lorry borne force was to drive straight into the Town and knock out all the police posts except Victoria Barracks, which was thought to be quite difficult to capture. A group on foot was to come into the Town by the back way through Likas and Signal Hill, and take post at the landward end of the old Customs, while the Islanders was to attack the town near Fraser Street. The signal for the assault of the Islanders was to be the sound of a bugles blown by the lorry-borne force after getting to grips with the enemy. As we have said earlier on, no one knows for certain what Kwok planned to do next. On the night of October, 9th was perfect for the attack.

Despite their well-organized spy system, the Japanese had not the slightest idea of what was coming and had arranged for a lecture at the Koa Club (the Jesselton Recreation Club) and all leading citizens were supposed to attend. The moon was nearing the full but there was some clouds which could gave the men cover. Kwok wore his American Army uniform, and the rest of his men wore dark clothing, except some who dressed in chawats (loincloth) and darkened their otherwise bare-bodies. The force had three lorries which were to take the party by road to Kota Kinabalu (Jesselton). They dowsed one headlight, showing only one as a sign for easy identification.

The first blow was struck at Tuaran where all the Japanese policemen were killed and seize six rifles with some ammunition and a much larger stock of shotgun ammunition. They returned with twelve heads. Next came the Japanese Police Station at Menggatal where the garrison of fifteen Japanese was wiped out. They also shot three local policemen. These two swift blows accounted for thirty enemy killed without any loss to the guerrillas. The two-pronged attacked on Kota Kinabalu, (Jesselton) now developed. The overland force made off for Likas and the lorries or Truck force prepared for its swoop down the road. Meantime, the sea raid was being prepared. For days the Islanders, comprising of Suluks, Binadans and Bajaus, had been gathering in their boats. From as far North as Mantanani Island, they came sailing at night to avoid Japanese detection. The Islanders mustered in their boats on the beaches of the off-shore islands near Kota Kinabalu (Jesselton), then moved in and stood off the sea wall ready for the attack, the pirate blood of their ancestors fully roused. It was too much to hope that the attack would be a complete surprise.

The alarm was given by a Taiwanese spy who ran in from Menggatal. The Japanese meeting broke up in confusion and many Japanese made their way to places of safety. But the truck borne fighters were soon in Town and attacking their first objective, the

Police Station on South Road. This post was supported by troops in the nearby military Post Office, and there were armed men in the Japanese Military Police post, in the Sports Club not far away, so the guerrillas had a difficult task.

They succeeded after a short and fierce battle. The Military Police did not interfere to assist their comrades. The guerrillas were disappointed because there was only a small stock of ammunition in the Police Station.

Bugle call gave the signal to the Islanders, and they stormed over the sea wall to attack. The party ordered to attack the Customs went in bent on death and destruction. They hurled flaming torches at the godowns - many of which were filled with rubber, and started fire which burnt and lasted for more than seven days.

It was quite unfortunate, that there were no Allied ships around, in the area. The Japanese guard ran frantically down the wharf towards the Town, but found their way blocked by the overland force who had arrived on time. The guard was instantly killed.

The second group of Islanders attacked along Fraser Street where there were many Japanese. These they sought out and killed. Some Japanese fled to Victoria Barracks at Batu Tiga. These were too strongly held, and the guerrillas wisely left them alone. Two Japanese started running and did not stop until they reached safety at Kinarut. One Japanese jumped into the sea and swam to Gaya Island, where he hid until the battle was over.

The Japanese Police Chief Ishikawa, also managed to escape but the Manager of the Japanese Nauri Company and his assistant were not so fortunate. Matnor was the Japanese Food Controller, who was dragged from his car and beheaded. The guerrillas assumed that anyone in a car or truck (except their own one-eyed vehicles) was enemy. Unfortunately, the Chinese driver of the Sanitary Board truck decided to escape in his vehicle. He and his newly-married wife were mistaken for Japanese and were both shot dead.

Lieutenant Albert Kwok issued two notices. One was a declaration of war against the Japanese. The other was an appeal to the public to help his men. Among other things, he asked the people not to offer his troops strong drink. He then gave orders for all his men to withdraw from Kota Kinabalu (Jesselton).

The Islanders took to their boats and the rest of the resistance fighters went back by road to Menggatal. They destroyed the bridge at Inanam to delay any pursuit. They need not have done so. The Japanese were so bewildered that they did not know what to do next. In all, the whole operation took exactly three hours. There were three black hours defeat for the Japanese and glorious victory for the men of courage for Sabah. (North Borneo)

The following morning, all the main buildings in Kota Kinabalu (Jesselton) right up to Tuaran, were fully decorated with flags to celebrate the Double Tenth (10th October). They were the Sabah Jack (North Borneo Union Jack) the Union Jack, the United States Stars and Stripes and the Chinese Flag. The people celebrated the feast in freedom.

Lieutenant Kwok's headquarters this day were at Mansiang near Menggatal and here the celebration was the gayest of them all. On 12th October, a small force under a colourful character called Rajah George, who is also known to his friends as Gringo, set out to capture Kota Belud. George was an ex-student of All Saints' School and a leading athlete. At Tengilan, they ran into three Japanese and after a short fight killed them. One of them was Ishikawa, the Japanese Police Chief who escaped on the night of the raid at Kota Kinabalu (Jesselton).

George telephoned Kota Belud and ordered the Japanese there to be arrested. He then rode into the Town clad in Iashikawa's riding boots, and wearing his samurai (Japanese sword). On his instructions the Japanese police were executed.

It was at Kota Belud that the pre-war detachment of the North Borneo Armed Constabulary fought the Japanese. The majority of these men were Dusuns/Kadazans from Tambunan and they put up a gallant fight against the Japanese. Two of the Volunteers lived throughout the war. They are Inspector Gubud and P.C. Cullah. Their comrades at arms lost their lives. Some died under torture and some died with their former officer, Mr. Charles Peter, at the infamous place of execution at Petagas.

October 13th bears an unlucky number, and this was the day the Japanese struck back. Troops and planes were rushed to Kota Kinabalu (Jesselton), and the villages along the Tuaran road were bombed and machine-gunned and later taken over by the Japanese troops. They were after any person who had assisted Lieutenant Kwok and his men, but they were not particular whom they punished, in their usual cruelty manner of handling the people. Many people fled in terror only to be rounded up like a herd of cattle, and blindly accused of helping the guerrillas, and then beaten and severely tortured.

Kwok and his men were forced back beyond the Tamparuli bridge to Ranau-Ranau, where they beat off an attack, but had to pull out to new positions. They kept up the fight but their ammunition stocks were low and they desperately needed supplies from the Philippines. He dared not move away into the hills and sever his connection with the Sulu Island. He was forced to remain within sight and sound of the sea. He expected the promised assistance to arrive any day but in the event, it did not arrive till December, two months later, when it was too late.

The attitude of the Natives during the first few days was cheerful for they had suffered much at the cruel hands of the Japanese, and they liked the sight of enemy blood. To despise life is the first qualification of a rebel. The path of revolt has never run smooth. Neither the Bajaus nor the Dusuns/Kadazans would tread this rough road. Without Native help the guerrillas failed to make headway and stood grimly on the defensive.

The Native farmers stood aside, did not join with the guerrillas and hurried to greet the Japanese reinforcements which soon arrived. The native farmer knows only too well that his interest lies with the winning party and no one is to be blamed.

Before long some of the band were losing hope and though they knew the terrible danger that lies ahead of them if they returned home, they wanted to be back with their families. Kwok allowed them to go and the remainder of the band made their way to Kiangsom near Inanam. Here they were attacked by the Japanese and scattered. Kwok and six of his men took refuge in the Shantung Chinese settlement near Penampang.

Chong Fu Kui, a shopkeeper at Donggongon, Penampang, visited them secretly and carefully pointed out that the place was too dangerous. He advised them to move elsewhere. The name of Chong Fu Kui has fallen into disrepute and he is regarded by many Chinese as little less than a traitor, but history will not judge him harshly.

Chong Fu Kui advised that the party should shift to the cemetery of Northern Chinese people which lies between the reservoir and Batu Tiga on the low ranges of hills intersected by steep hills and valleys. The evil spirits who are supposed to haunt such places would help to keep unwelcome visitor away.

This move brought the party a mile closer to the Japanese Headquarters, and Batu Tiga lay only two and a half miles away to the West, but the decision was sound, and there under the guardianship of the ghosts they spent several days, in a gravedigger's hut. Though very uncomfortable, the hiding place was secure.

Then an unfortunate but typical incident occurred. A gambler staked and lost in an evil hour the money given to him for purchase of supplies for the refugees. The man acted as a messenger between them and Chong Fu Kui. He was an inveterate gambler and he lost the sum of two hundred dollars which Chong Fu Kui has placed in his hands for Lieutenant Kwok. There is no gambling in which the devil has not a share and the man foolishly returned to Chong Fu Kui and tried to force him to replace the lost sum. Chong Fu Kui protested. The man threatened exposure to the Japanese, involving Chong Fu Kui and the lives of all the refugees.

Voices were raised in anger and a spy in the pay of the Japanese moved a little closer under cover of darkness of the shop verandah to overhear. Chong Fu Kui under the threat of exposure agreed to support the refugees further, took more money from the safe and the excitement subsided. But a mischief has been done and the Japanese spy, who had lived for long among the Northern Chinese and knew something of their language, hurried to report to his cruel village Headman, Majakui, who in turn reported the story to the Japanese. Enquiries were set a foot and Majakui was ordered by the Japanese to produce the rebels under pain of death. They were hiding in his village jurisdiction and he was held responsible.

Chong Fu Kui also heard rumours of approaching trouble and acted with his usual promptitude. He led the refugees from the cemetery a mile or more further inland and hid them again in the valleys at the foot of the range of hills. He moved them from place to place each day and he knew their whereabouts. Even then it was not too late for the refugees to retire to the mountains, but definite news had been received at last that the reinforcements from the Philippines were on the way. The guerillas expected them daily and clung to the coast.

Meanwhile both Majakui and Chong Fu Kui were under great pressure from the Japanese and the end was near. At 4.00 a.m. on 19th December 1943 over 100 Japanese soldiers set out from Batu Tiga and surrounded the area before sunrise. Majakui and Chong Fu

Kui were given a short notice to produce the refugees and in default, they and all the inhabitants of the area would be shot.

The Japanese hesitated to come to close quarters with the guerrillas, who were well armed. Chong Fu Kui undertook the hazardous attempt to persuade Lieutenant Kwok and his men to surrender. He went alone into the valley, while the Japanese held off at a distance. The Japanese certainly feared that the guerrillas would fight to the last and that there would be many casualties in the bush fight.

By 10.00 a.m. Chong Fu Kui had persuaded Lieutenant Kwok and his men to surrender to save the lives of the inhabitants of the valley. Lieutenant Kwok realised that further resistance would be useless and he decided to surrender to the enemy. By taking all responsibility upon himself he hoped to save further loss of life and the persecution of the people.

The delay in the arrival of the long promised and awaited reinforcements had filled him with foreboding. His faith had faltered. His men had searched the horizon in vain. Silence broaded on the face of the sea. He gave up. In this particular hour, whatever his faults, he possessed the greatest of all qualities, which is courage in adversity.

Lao Tzu (600B.C.) quote – "When you are no longer fit to hold a position do not be tempted by greed or pride to continue in it, but rather retire while your energies are still active."

Lieutenant Kwok was fit enough, but a revolt that stands still is a revolt that is ruined. His plans had failed and he did not hesitate to follow the heavenly rule and to retire for the sake of the people of North Borneo (Sabah). That old Chinese philosopher had a dry and grim humour and often he chuck bitterly in his thin beard at the frailties of human nature.

Disappointment clogged the guerrillas spirit and their hearts failed them. They might have fought their way to the hills and sold their lives dearly, and such a determination would have cost the enemy much in pursuit. Instead Lieutenant Kwok surrendered with his weapons to the Japanese whom he had opposed so long in Sulu and North Borneo. For two solid years the guiding principle of his life, to oppose the enemy, had remained consistent. His practice had matched his principle. The end had now come.

Lieutenant Kwok and his men followed Chong Fu Kui from their hideout in the hills out to the Penampang Road and there they were presented to the Japanese officer in command. He was waiting on the roadside about four miles out of Jesselton (Kota Kinabalu) at the top of the rise where there was a small hamlet of one or two shops.

The refugees were taken into custody and marched to the Jesselton Hotel, where they were handed over to the military authorities. They were photographed repeatedly by their captors and were sent to the offices of the infamous Kempeitai in the Jesselton Sports Club.

There Lieutenant Kwok was put to every form of torture. Those in prison with him, who have survived, say that he suffered quietly and flatly refused to answer any questions put to him. He made his own statement saying that he was the sole cause and alone was responsible for the Double Tenth revolt. He tried to commit suicide, but the attempt failed.

After suffering bitterly for two or three weeks he was sent to Batu Tiga prison to await the mass execution which took place at Petagas a few days later in January.

Of the others who took part in these last days of the Kinabalu Guerillas, Chong Fu Kui discredited and disgraced in the view of his fellows left the country as soon as he could and return to China. Chong Fu Kui did not in fact return to China. He took refuge in the forests of the East Coast working in timber camps. After some fifteen years he emerged from the forests and returned to his home at Mile 5 Penampang Road, where he received a warm welcome.

The Village Headman – Majakui Bin Salaman was arrested, put on trial by a Military Court after the return of the British. There was a long list of charges against Majakui for collaborating with the Japanese and he was sentence to death on the specific charge of spearing to death two Chinese who were sheltering in a ditch after the Revolt of the Double Tenth. Majakui admitted the charges, but pleaded that he was drunk with tapai (intoxicating rice wine) at that time. The defence was not accepted by the Court and he was convicted of murder. Majakui Bin Salaman was sentenced to death on 5th January, 1946. The sentenced was confirmed by the Supreme Commander South East Asia on 21st January, and he was hanged at Batu Tiga a few days later. He was not charged with the betrayal of Lieutenant Kwoks's place of refuge.

The Japanese arrested many people, both townsfolk and Islanders. On 24th January, 1944 they decided to finished them off. They condemned a hundred and seventy-six of these to death, and a hundred and thirty-one was transferred to Labuan. Of the total number of prisoners arrested by the Japanese only nine remained alive at the end of the War to tell us their horrible experiences under the Rising Sun Government, who ruled Sabah, (North Borneo) from January, 1942 to October 1945. At 3.00 a.m. on the 21st January 1944 the condemned men were pushed into cattle trucks and taken to Petagas. The Japanese blocked the road to the village for three days for fear of being attacked by the people.

At Petagas Lieutenant Albert Kwok, Charles Peter, Chen Chau Kong, Kong Tse Phui and Li Tet Phui were made to stand in a row and photographed. They were then beheaded by the Japanese. The rest of the doomed men which includes Jules Stephens, Panglima Ali, and Rajah George Sinnadurai, were killed by machine gun fire and their bodies were thrown into long trenches already dug few days in advance before the mass execution.

There is now a Memorial Garden built on the spot where the execution was carried out, and every year on the anniversary of the executions, there is a religious service to honour those brave men who died for the love of their country.

The Japanese did not carry out their plan to take Chinese youths into the Japanese Armed Forces and Chinese girls as prostitutes for the Japanese army. As it was, they made the people of Sabah (North Borneo) pay heavily for the few hours of freedom. The career of the Kinabalu Guerrillas was ended but the guerrilla warfare went on under Ex-Chief Inspector Duallis, a pensioner of the North Borneo Armed Constabulary and a Peluan Murut.

To the honour of the Muruts, let it be mentioned that there was not a single case of collaborating with the Japanese during the whole period of the occupation.

In their warfare they were inspired by the stories which reached them from the West Coast Residency. The Muruts waged their warfare until the Allied Armies arrived upon the scene. Ex-Chief Inspector Duallis lived to a happy old age and died in May, 1949, amongst the hills in his village where he had served so well and for a long time.

6

Japanese Atrocities –
During the Occupation in Sabah
(North Borneo)

World War Two meant many things to many people. To over 50,000,000 men, women and children, it meant death. To hundreds of millions more in the occupied areas and theaters of combat, the war meant hell on earth. Suffering and grief, often with little if any awareness of a cause or reason beyond the terrifying events of the moment.

To the nations of the world, World War Two meant technological innovation, bureaucratic expansion, and an extraordinary mobilization of human resources and ideological fervor. Governments on all sides presented the conflict as a holy war for national survival and glory, a mission to defend and propagate the finest values of their state and culture. Many individual gave their lives in the belief that they were sacrificing themselves for such ideals.

The Guerrilla attacks on Tuaran, Menggatal and Jesselton (Kota Kinabalu) petered out at midnight and early the following morning, prompted the Japanese to retaliate by taking action to meet these flagrant acts of defiance.

On the 14th October the Japanese struck back, several Japanese planes flew from Kuching, Sarawak, to Kota Kinabalu, (Jesselton) and began bombing the towns and villages. Both Tuaran and Kota Belud were heavily bombed and many buildings were destroyed. Whenever the planes sighted people, they machine-gunned them. At Tuaran, many people took to their boats on the river endeavouring to escape from the scene, but planes dived towards them and machine-gunned them. In some cases they dropped bombs on boats in the river.

The settlers and their families were rounded up and many others who were resident of Tuaran district. Women and children were accommodated under the floor of the Tuaran District office, sleeping and squatting between the posts. The men, mostly old and sick, were made to lie under the burning sun or in pelting rain on the open football field. The men describe this treatment as "Kena jemur macam ikan masin", dried in the sun like salted fish. At night the men were herded into the small prison. A handful of rice was given to each as his or her ration. After two to three days of continued investigation those who could prove that they had not taken part in the revolt were allowed to return home with their families to their village with the good citizen badges. Nobody escaped the ordeal.

Japanese soldiers arrived in large numbers and rounded up groups of people, including, Bajaus, Dusuns/Kadazans and Chinese, tying them up, and beating them causing much suffering. Many houses were burned down, particularly when the owners had fled at the approach of Japanese. The Japanese Commander rounded up all the Village Headmen and police ordered them to search the countryside for refugees. The search parties were divided into two groups. One group searched for the guerrillas and their supporters and was composed of Japanese soldiers and Kempeitei, with few, if any Native or Chinese collaborators. The other group searched for the bodies of the dead Japanese and was composed of Japanese soldiers, Native police and others.

Between 65-70 percent of the newly recruited Native police force under the orders of the Japanese took part in these searches, a few of them behaved brutally like the Japanese. Their misdeeds were remembered and they were subsequently brought to trial three years later. This grim period lasted for slightly over six months. The Japanese members of these search parties showed no mercy to the people and behaved with great brutality. All the Chinese in the villages outside (Kota Kinabalu) Jesselton and more particularly at Inanam, Menggatal, Telipok and Tuaran were arrested whether they possessed fire-arms or not. If any of them showed resistance or try to run away, they would be executed on the spot.

The news of the arrests soon spread and many of the people scattered into the forests, but the search parties went after them, and if they found any refugees they murdered them. At Tuaran many of the Chinese assembled on the bank of the Tuaran River. There, the search parties arrived, the people were bound hands and feet. They were all beheaded and their bodies were thrown into the river.

A good citizen badge was issued to those whose action could stand the test of enquiry. The badge consisted of a small piece of cloth cut into a square two or three inches each way. Chinese characters were stamped on it in black ink and these read – West Coast Civil Administrators Seal. This was pinned to the chest of the man who had been cleared by Japanese authority. The badge is his life preserver.

The people were quick to turn these badges to their own advantage. They were passed from hand to hand and pinned to the chest of those who needed them most. These small badges of cloth could easily be copied or duplicated. Those who stayed at home were slow to apply for the badge for their own interest or safety, while the guerrillas had more than a dozen with them. It was an opportunity for the trial of wits and the Chinese were not the losers.

Many guerrillas made full use of these badges to return home and to move around on their warfare. Many live today, thanks to God.

Andrew Wong, a teacher of All Saints' School, Kota Kinabalu, (Jesselton) who is also a well known Scoutsmaster, took to the hill with other guerrillas and lived in the Dusun/

Kadazan villages at Ranau and Bundu Tuhan area, South of Mount Kinabalu. Their presence was soon discovered and reported by Dusun/Kadazan collaborators to the Japanese in Keningau. Sergeant Fara Singh (a Sheik), formerly attached to the North Borneo Armed Constabulary who had continued his service with the Japanese was ordered by the Japanese to arrest them.

Andrew Wong and his small party were then at Kitai village halfway between Randagung and Ranau. Sergeant Fara Singh with about half a dozen native policeman (Jikidan) made contact with the local Dusun/Kadazan Headman and wisely persuaded them to capture the whole party. This was an easy task, because Andrew Wong trusted his Dusun/Kadazan hosts, in whose house he was living and whose hospitality he had accepted. The Dusuns/Kadazans overpowered the Chinese youths on watch and captured all of them. The Chinese had only an air-rifle and a few parangs between them. Fara Singh ordered the Dusuns/Kadazans to dig graves and set the Chinese tied hand and foot in a row squatting beside the graves. The dirty minded Sergeant assigned a living target for each constable to shoot at. The Dusun/Kadazan police loaded their rifles and at the command of Sergeant Fara Singh, fired a volley of shots.

As two or three Chinese were still alive, a second volley was fired. Two of the Dusun/Kadazan Jikidan swore that they had fired into the air and not at the Chinese. The Chinese were not bandits. Andrew Wong's companions were Lo Yin Fah of Tuaran Estate, and his two sons Lo Vui En of the Treasury Department and Lo Vui Nyen of the Lands & Surveys Department, Kota Kinabalu (Jesselton). The other gentleman was Chong Tet, a businessman from Tuaran. Fara Singh had the authority to arrest, but has no right to be a judge and an executioner at the same time, by taking the laws into his own hand. His commanding officer, a Japanese remained all the time at Randagung, which is half-a-day's walk on foot from Kitai awaiting Fara Singh's return.

The Chinese made no resistance when they were captured. There was not even a semblance of enquiry or trial, but instead, massacre followed immediately.

In 1946 Fara Singh was arrested and tried for murder. The trial took place at Keningau before a Military Court, presided by Senior Civil Affairs Officer in charge of the Interior as the Superior Military Court Judge. The Military Court found Fara Singh guilty and sentenced him to death. The judge reported that the prisoner had not been able to get counsel for his defence to visit so out of the way a place as Keningau, in the Interior of North Borneo.

The prisoner pleaded Japanese orders as a defence. But the order of a superior does not relieve a subordinate from responsibility if the subordinate knows that by carrying out orders he is committing a crime. The fact of an order may mitigate the punishment but it does not affect the responsibility. Fara Singh's case caused repercussions as far as India, whose Government asked for a re-trial, and in pursuance of its policy to defend any of its nationals who were charged with collaboration in South East Asia, expended large sums of money on his legal defence. He was again convicted and sentenced to death and yet on hearing the appeal, the sentence was upheld. Following the result of the appeal, the Colony Government committed the sentence to 15 years imprisonment.

When Fara Singh was still serving his sentence in jail, his wife married a Murut prison warden called Eram, and had many children including that of Fara Singh's own children, before she married Eram. The family is now living at Kampong Karamatoi, Sook, Keningau.

When Fara Singh was discharged from prison, he worked as a Mandor in one of the Stone quarry Company at Labuan. Fara Singh died just before the formation of Malaysia in the early sixties.

At the Coast several hundreds of people were remanded and transported to Batu Tiga for enquiry and trial. They were subjected to the most brutal treatment and many died.

One of the eye witnesses described a true scene at the prison involving a Kapitan China of Penampang called Yu Eh, he was crushed under stones weighing three to four hundred pounds and sustained two broken ribs. A policeman pierced the side of his body with a knife when he could not speak. His final interrogation was made when he was laid in a coffin and it was made obvious to him that his days is numbered. In view of this, he maintained his courageous attitude, and admitted nothing. After two weeks of continuous torture of every sort he was set free. Yu Eh had in fact donated two thousand dollars to the Kinabalu Guerrilla's fund.

The Japanese continued its torture even during broad daylight. During the night Chinese under investigation were brought out of the prison and beaten on their heads with heavy clubs until they died. Chinese Towkays from Keningau who were tortured and finally beaten to death by the Japanese were Ah Tan, Ah Hui and Fung Goon Kee or better known by the people of Keningau as Ang Goon. The corpses of those beaten to death by the Japanese were visible to all eye witnesses, that as a result of the beating blood had oozed from the mouths, eyes, ears and noses. Their brains were smashed and their eyes gouged out. Their tongues protruded. The corpses of these emaciated sufferers were put into coffins, four or five corpses in each coffin, and carried away.

In some cases, the victims were nailed to boards by spikes driven through the palms of their hands, like Jesus Christ nailed to the cross. Scores of men were slung from roof beams by ropes tied to their hands and feet, and as their bodies wilted, their fellow prisoners with grim humor referred to them as "Ikan Masin", salted fish. After the war, full enquiries and statements were made by the British Military authorities regarding the torture inflicted upon these innocent and unfortunate captives, and the evidence available shows that the cruelty was inflicted by the hands of the Japanese Kempeitai, and not by the locals.

An onlooker said the Japanese have three different ways of beheading prisoners, which he and other spectators had personally witnessed on the execution site. The Japanese officials, the fierce and hard-faced soldiers, the victims with their arms fully tied and trussed back and their shirts removed, is pushed forward one at a time. A Japanese officer (the executioner) draws his sword with a sharp whirr of solid steel and steps up to the man. Then wheeling it round his head with two hands upon the long hilt, he sweeps it. A sudden, sullen thump, a chocking whistling sound, the head is detached from the body. The officer wipes his sword on the short hand turf, and steps aside for the next officer, that he too may taste blood.

The second method is the victim would be forced to kneel down with his hands tied at his back and his head bowed. His head was then struck off. At Sandakan during a round-up of the people on one of the Islands, a Chinese girl was forced on her knees and one of the Jikidan (Native police) rose and with his parang struck her a blow across the neck. He thought he had killed her, but she lived at God's will and eventually appeared in Court after the war as a witness against her assailant and others on charge of murder. The Jikidan was found guilty and hanged to death.

The third method of beheading, the victim was bound with his hands behind his back and stood up. The Japanese executioner, often an officer who is proud of his killing skill made a short harangue to the people assembled and swinging the double-handed sword (samurai) in a circular sweep struck off the victim's head with a blow.

In another method of execution which is not decapitation, was to split the victim's head downwards with a sword blade. The Japanese samurai swords were heavy and the handles were long, so that the swords were wielded with both hands. When several prisoners were to be beheaded all at the same time, a large trench was dug. The prisoners were led out in single file with their hands tied behind their backs. As each one of them approached the edge of the trench in turn, he was caused to kneel with bowed head which was struck off. Both head and body were kicked down into the trench and buried there with the others who were executed together.

After the failure of the Double Tenth Revolt, Dr. Lau Lai and Cheah Loong Ghee were arrested by the Japanese on suspicion of planning for a second revolt. They were caught and interrogated separately. Dr. Lau Lai was severely tortured by the Japanese for twelve solid days, when he gave way after every fibre of resistance had been drained out from him, the Japanese hanged Dr. Lau Lai with another man, the same morning at Batu Tiga.

Cheah Loong Ghee received a similar treatment. His refusal to speak was absolute. He said nothing under the most terrible torture, and steadfastly refused to reveal any information whatsoever. Few men have been through such ill treatment and retained their power of control. Not a single name or secret was ever dragged from his tongue. Though pieces of his flesh were sliced from his body and held before his eyes under threat that more will be cut if he refused to speak. He still refused to say anything. Cheah Loong Ghee died suffering greatly in the prison in 1944.

On the 5th May, 1944 at 1000 hrs there was another mass execution, at Batu Tiga prison. More than twenty Japanese military officers went into the prison, brought out many Chinese and Dusun/Kadazan prisoners, bound them, tortured them by burning their flesh with embers, and having failed to force them to speak and admit their suspected offence, sent them out for execution.

To the everlasting disgrace of the Japanese Administration in Sabah (North Borneo), its officers had successfully converted Batu Tiga prison into a butcher's shambles.

The wives of the condemned leaders were fortunately not punished. The women upheld the prestige of their men, and whatever they knew to the contrary they regarded it as

The remains of the Japanese Torture Cell in one of the nearby islands, near Jesselton (Kota Kinabalu)

their duty to shield the facts from the enemy. One of the woman said she was not afraid of what the Japanese might do to her, but she is afraid of what they might do to her children. I always feared that they might take my children away. There was something triumphant in this spirit and it has been seen that at least the sacrifice of the men and the courage of the women achieved success and kept the children safe from harm. The men of today may not know of the bravery of the women of yesterday.

Meanwhile, the Japanese knew that the Islanders from Mantanani, Gaya, Udar, Sepangar, Sinjatan, Memutik, Manukan, Dinawan and Pulau Tiga, were involved in the Double Tenth Revolt of the Kinabalu Guerrillas and had attacked Japanese military stations. In retaliation they arrested their Headman Panglima Ali, of Suluk Island, and confined him in the prison at Batu Tiga.

Fourteen days later Suluk Island was raided by Japanese soldiers and Native Jikidans. The Japanese machine-gunned the inhabitants of the island and setting fire to all the houses on the island. The men were shot as they come running out from their houses.

Some of the islanders put up a fight against the Japanese and wounded quite a few of them. The Japanese soon overcame the resistance and killed all the men whom they could find. Of the total inhabitants in the island, 54 were killed 60 survived. 30 women and children were removed to Bongawan and of these 25 died of malnutrition and ill treatment.

At Udar island, opposite Menggatal river, the Japanese carried out a similar massacre. Of the 64 people living on the island, 29 were killed and 35 survived, 15 women and children were sent to Bongawan to work in the Japanese rice fields.

At Dinawan Island all the males were arrested and taken to Batu Tiga prison. Few days later they were taken back to Dinawan Island, where they were executed by machine-gun fire in the presence of their wives and children. Some of the women were imprisoned. Only a few of them survived to tell us the tale of their horrible treatment. Some of the women were pricked by bayonets in the womb until they died. The Suluk Chief was executed with the other prisoners at the infamous place of execution, PETAGAS.

The Japanese continued their killings from Island to Island. Known for their cruelty, faggots were applied to the bodies of the islanders and their hair was set alight. Many more died as a result of this cruel treatment. Women and children were gunned down, and those who were wounded were shot with pistols to ensure that their lives were ended. On another island the Japanese rounded up all the women and children, and after removing their money and jewellery, strung them together on a rope, fastened to the post of a Surau, (Muslim Prayer House) and mowed them down with machine-gun fire, killing all of them.

In Sabah (North Borneo) and in other invaded countries, Japan professed to have come to liberate the Asians from their European or American oppressors and to incorporate their country into a sphere of co-prosperity and equality, six weeks after the bombing of Pearl Harbour, General Tojo described Japan's East Asia Co-Prosperity Sphere as a great undertaking, which will mark a new epoch in the annals of mankind, in which

The main entrance to the War Memorial garden at Petagas, Jesselton, (Kota Kinabalu)

The Petagas War Memorial garden where hundreds of people including men, women and children were massacred by the Japanese during the war.

Japan will proceed to construct a new world order along with the Allies in Europe. Instead of equality or prosperity, North Borneo, which had long enjoyed peace, was subjected to an oppressive regime which brought misery and death.

Civilians, including some of the Natives were massacred as were the Australian prisoners of war in Japanese custody. The worse and most infamous of these atrocities was the brutal extermination of almost all the Sandakan Prisoners of War which occurred over three years and involved many Japanese.

To the people of Sabah (North Borneo) it was very apparent that the so called Co-Prosperity Sphere was no partnership but a one-way traffic affair in the Japanese direction.

Many hundreds of Japanese officers and others in the rank and file were subsequently brought to trial and convicted. Their punishment included death by hanging, death by firing squad, or life time imprisonment.

Let this be a lesson to all of us in Sabah, that upsetting the constitution and the laws, and ignoring the right of the people is dangerous, and not beneficial to the future and well being of the Nation.

THE WAR MONUMENT IN
KENINGAU NEAR THE AIRPORT

This memorial was erected as a result of Colony wide donations collections of which was organised by all Chinese Chamber of Commerce in memory of those whose names appear below. They suffered imprisonment, great hardships and ultimately death near this spot during World War II.

1 CHO HUAN LAI
  CONSUL FOR THE REPUBLIC OF CHINA.
2 C.D. LE GROS CLARK
  CHIEF SECRETARY SARAWAK
3 V.A. STOOKES
  MEDICAL PRACTITIONER, SANDAKAN.
4 W.H. WEBBER
  CIVIL ENGINEER, MANILA, PHILIPPINES.
5 D. MACDONALD
  PLANTER, KUCHING, SARAWAK.

Donations were also received from the Governments of Sarawak and North Borneo and relatives of the deceased.

FORMER DIGGERS CLAIM JAPANESE ATE AUSSIE SOLDIERS

POWs seek compo over war horrors

U-BUILD GAR...

A group of Australian prisoners-of-war with artificial legs made in Changi   compensation claim

tarvation a efence for cannibalism: ex-war chief

TOKYO.— A former Japanese army chief in New Guinea yesterday said he never heard of atrocities against Australian troops "although one Japanese soldier was found guilty in a post-war trial at Wewak for his involvement in cannibalism."

Kengoro Tanaka, who was the chief of strategic staff in New Guinea, said the soldier's initial death sentence was reduced to five years' prison cause near-starvation gener was accepted as a def against such charges.

An Australian Gove report of 43 years ag public last week, said troops were so hungr ate the bodies of Au diers in New Gui the flesh of their o

The report, de anese newspap also said Ja beheaded A men, raped and missi bound ca practice Such Webb natio Toky in

book writer decided whether to include a newly found document on past history. Government officials vetted textbooks for sch... use.

Former Diggers claimed Japanese troops had ten Australians, and 1 any idea of Australi being prosecuted for crimes was unthink-

...ical of the feelings still linger was a ... by Stan Nichol-... Sydney, who said the bodies of Aus... roops which had ... tially stripped of the flesh wrap-...n leaves

... soldier Norrie ... he saw the ... ldier who had ... ed and hung ... very deftly ... obviously

Both bodies were armless, and from the thighs and legs the Japanese had cut large pieces.

The Australians found the remnants wrapped in leaves.

In the diary of Japanese lieutenant Sakamoto who died in battle interpreters found the following

Because of the food shortage some companies have been eating the flesh of Australian soldiers. The taste is said to be good.

Another captured diary written by a soldier of a machine gun company stated ... No provisions ...re said to be eating

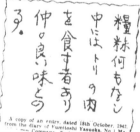

A copy of an entry, dated 18th October, 1942 from the diary of Fumitoshi Yasuoka, No 1 Ma... ... Company, Tsukamoto Battalion. The

糧秣何もなし中にはトリの肉を食す者あり仲の良い味とう

1942: AUG 26 - SEPT 6 Japanese land-raid at Milne Bay Australian prisoners tortured and murdered

NEW GUINEA ... CORAL SEA

I just cannot forget, says soldier who witnessed atrocitie

By NICKI BYRNE

... be said he wanted to forget but could not.

He said there had been no warning behind their atrocities, no reasonable explanation to be remembered that had happened.

Three memories were with him most vividly and he will never be able to shake free the release of the Japanese surrender.

... martialled by Japanese serviceman at Milne Bay.

... Whippet who was raped and killed by ... immortal bystanders.

... Mr. Macdonald, of Burden [a Betts Roo, which headed at Milne Bay.

... He paid the ...

... heard those army commander that soldiers had ... Japanese camp remembered as the ... what they had seen, were proper that he ... the truth, the native wares well and ... murdered, their bayonets cut off and ... regret," he said

... but only did it happen on the

RSL to support ban on Japan if war claim fails

By SID MAHER and NICKI BYRNE

The ... and ... League will back a planned trade boycott against Japan unless a $10,000 million ... gency claim for co... atrocities is to be ...

Anzac Presidents of W... Branch a high sources representing a high-ranking Australian ex-POWs, called for the ban ... its members' claimed for war compensation would a...

The intention of a spoke... Bowman, chairman, Mr. David ... Barrett, the spokesman for the release of the 1945 list of the POWs, who the half Japanese ... Japanese camps traditional and cannibalism, torture ... settlement during World

The RSL national president said that Australians not the Japanese did not accept fate, and with the exception of Japanese companies before the not do to represent an but did not approve it ... by the Japanese the for Japanese Government ...

and North Vietnam for some to try and trade with the...

claim should be considered legally even in Japanese ... By ... of two ... Bigadier Garland sale will come ... of POWs of former families who had suffered during the ... organised memorial respect of the RSL Queensland servicemen ... used the RSL Raymond but said a letter of issue be the motion would go before the annual National Human Rights Commission within six months.

Mr Barrett told the Webb Report requested by the Webb in William Webb, ... a small portion of the half thing else should be clearly killed all million peo...

...the Webb Report would have say heinally in Australians ... found it disgusting and ... "Whether it would help to know ...

... about ... the world's army trade to have with each other on a different

"This will only confirm what a lot of people thought hap proud of their many people wondering how these people died

"It will generate an atmos ghers that would have been left."

Sir Albert said at a time when there was a lot of discus ment in our Japanese invest ment in Australia the report ... feelings

"I have no doubts about the Webb ... of publishing that the Jap's a criminal trade dependency with that will affect a lot of people," he said

Brigadier Garland of ... release of the list of ...

7

The Liberation of Sabah (North Borneo)

After the death of Lieutenant Albert Kwok and his band of Courageous Sabahans, the Guerrilla warfare continued in Sabah (North Borneo) until the Japanese were defeated. After the Double Tenth Revolt, the Japanese did not made any attempt to collect taxes from the people of Sabah, either by way of rent or poll tax. By forcing the Japanese to give up their efforts to coerce the people into some form of conscription, either for military service, prostitution or labour, and the cancellation of all kinds of taxes, the Revolt caused changes in the condition of the people, and as a result of what transpired, the Japanese realised that there was a limit beyond which they dared not go, and that there must be some lessening of the coercion of the inhabitants. They also learned that the people would not stand being bullied continuously without hitting back.

The revolt also led to movements of Japanese troops. The garrison was maintained at approximately 25,000 men and the General in command of the Japanese Armed Forces in Borneo moved his headquarters from Kuching, State of Sarawak, to Kota Kinabalu (Jesselton) and later to Sapong, Tenom, to await further developments.

The revolt in general showed that the spirit of the people was very much alive, and it lived until the coming of the Allied Forces. The North Borneo Kinabalu Guerrillas was the only underground movement in Sabah (North Borneo). Although it failed, the people did not give up hope, on the contrary, it encouraged the formation of other bands.

The Japanese looked upon the North Borneo Kinabalu Guerrillas as Communists, but they looked upon their successors as Bandits. The Japanese admitted that there were considerable number of casualties amongst the troops as a result of Bandit activities. The Allies landed small groups of soldiers, who were assisted by the local people to carry out raids against the Japanese, and to send back information. The Natives on the otherhand, took an increasing share in harassing the enemy.

From June, 1944 to June, 1945 the Japanese in Sabah (North Borneo) began to feel that they had lost the war.

The Allies were fast approaching. The Japanese decided to move a large number of prisoners of war from Sandakan to Ranau, by forcing them on a march over the rugged country between these two Districts. The prisoners of war had been underfed, but positively overworked for years, and on their way to Ranau, they were given hardly any food

A plaque put up at the Kundasang War Memorial in honour of the Death March 1944-1945

The War Memorial Garden of Kundasang

Wreakages of some of the Japanese Zero Fighters and Bombers, shot down during the Second World War, at Keningau Airfield.

The Memorial Stone at Labuan Island to commemorate the landing of the 9th Division Australian Imperial Forces (10th June 1945) which led to the liberation of British North Borneo (Sabah) from the Japanese.

to eat, in which case, most of them died on these journeys, which were called "THE DEAD MARCH". There were three dead marches between January and May, 1945.

In commemoration of the Death March, the Government of Australia constructed a Memorial Garden, at Kundasang, Ranau, after the war dedicated to the memory of the 1,800 Australians, 600 British Servicemen who perished in the cruel hands of the Japanese, in the prisoner of war camps in Sandakan, and in the three forced marches from Sandakan to Ranau, and the many Sabahans who suffered death in trying to assist them.

In January, 1945 the Allies started bombing Sabah (North Borneo) in an attempt to break the enemy's will to fight. In May, 1945 Sandakan was heavily bombarded from the air and sea. This enraged the Japanese very much and they set fire to most of the buildings in Town. Kudat was flattened, and Kota Kinabalu (Jesselton) was attacked.

In June, 1945 the Australian Ninth Division landed and captured Labuan. The 9th Division was commanded by Major General G.F. Wooten, and its shoulder badge was a "T" which means Tobruk in North Africa because this was the 9th Division that had fought there with success and honour. The "T" can be seen on the sail of the ship in the old Sabah Coat of Arms. It has been placed there to show that the people honour the Australians who fought the enemy and liberated them from Japanese rule.

The Australians were assisted by forces already in Sabah (North Borneo) under the Command of Allied Officers, including Mr. R.G.P.N. Combe, later Resident of West Coast and Stipendiary Magistrate, Brunei Town in 1956, Major Rex Blow and Tom Harrisons, later Curator of Sarawak Museum. The local leaders were also in the fight against the Japanese , they were Tun Datu Haji Mustapha Bin Datu Harun, KVO., OBE, Datuk Haji Mohamad Yasin Bin Haji Hashim, OBE, Ex Sergeant Sulom Bin Gambias, of Keningau, Ex Sergeant Sumporoh of Ranau, and Ex Sergeant Garukon of Kampong Dangulad, Keningau.

The main centre for the Japanese Army was Sapong Estate in Tenom District. The Japanese Commander was General Baba, and he had approximately 25,000 men under his command. During the fighting around Rayoh and Beaufort, an Australian soldier won the highest British Military award for bravery, the Victoria Cross. He was Private T. Starcevitch, and there is a memorial erected in his honour in front of the Police Station at Beaufort.

The story of Australian soldier Leslie Thomas Starcevich, V.C. is significant to Sabah. This is because he was the recipient of World War Two's last Victoria Cross – the highest in the British Armed Forces.

Mr. Stanley Toomey, Starcevich's ex-comrade who came to Sabah in June, 1990 specifically to insert a plaque at the Beaufort memorial stone dedicated to Starcevich, said what the memorial stone stood for was clear to every visitor because every words was clearly engraved on the big plaque which read as follows: –

In June, 1945, on this hill, by his valour and disregard of danger, Private L.T. Starcevich

A monument put up by the people of Beaufort, in honour of Private LESLIE THOMAS STARCEVICH, V.C. of the 2/43 RD BATTALION A.I.F. who won the highest British Military award, the Victoria Cross, for routing the Japanese defenders single handed, at Beaufort, North Borneo (Sabah) in June, 1945.

of 2/43rd Battalion A.I.F. (Australian Imperial Forces), routed the Japanese defenders single handed for which he was awarded the Victoria Cross.

However, one big mystry which left many people wondering was what happened to Starcevich. In fact, the memorial stone, which has been there for years, made many assumed it was dedicated to the dead. But we know now that Starcevich died in November, 1989. The other question is who erected the Memorial Stone? The memorial stone was originally erected by the people of Beaufort in gratitude to the Australians for liberating them from the oppresive rule of the Japanese and the plaque dedicated to Starcevich was inserted only later.

Now that Starcevich had died the people should no longer be left wondering. It is a known fact that many of the members of the 2/43rd Battalion are still alive. In fact, there exists the 2/43rd Battalion Association which has a membership of approximately 150 who still hold a reunion every year, particularly on ANZAC Day.

Following Mr. Stanley Toomey's suggestion, the Association decided to sponsor an obituary plaque which was brought over to Sabah in June, 1990 and inserted. The epitaph reads:

> Vale (Farewell)
> Leslie Thomas Starcevich (VC)
> Born 5-9-1918 Died 17-11-1989
> Grass Patch West Australia
> Aged 71 years
> Lest We Forget
> 2/43 BN Association

While the memorial is dedicated specifically to Starcevich, in a bigger sense, it represents a special bond, a great feeling between the people of Beaufort and Sabah in general, and the 2/43rd Battalion from the 24th Brigade, Australian 9th Division.

The war finally ended when the Americans dropped the Atomic Bombs at Hiroshima and Nagasaki, on 6th and 9th August, 1945. The Atomic Bomb was dropped at a height of 29,333.1 ft. from a four-engine Superfortress B-29 Bomber named the "Enola Gay", and piloted by U.S. Air Force Colonel, Paul Tibbetts.

It was then the turn of the Japanese for a death march. The 6,000 Japanese troops at Pensiangan set off to a march from Pensiangan to Keningau and to march northwards to Beaufort to surrender to the Australians. They marched fully armed, but this time the Muruts were masters of the route which extended for 214 miles away, they were continually attacked by the Muruts, and many died. What is known is the condition of the few survivors who reached the camps on the railway sidings.

The Camp at Saliwangan, mile 64, another at mile 66, and a third at Hologilat, mile 69, were the end of the chain of rest camps extending from Pensiangan.

Death and dying spread out the whole way. These rest camps were at the Beaufort end

The Japanese surrendered to the Allied Forces in Singapore on the 12th September, 1945.

The author-fourth from the right squatting with members of the Sabah Field Force, guarding the unexplode bomb before the arrival of the Army Bomb Disposal Unit, to' defuse the Bomb.

The unexploded World War Two bomb, found at Liawan river Keningau.

of the long march, and they could accommodate only 400 survivors at a time. When the Japanese surrendered on the 9th September, 1945, the survivors were suffering from wounds, severe exhaustion and all kinds of tropical disease. It was indeed a death march for the Japanese.

Sabah (North Borneo) was finally liberated by the Allied Forces from the Rising Sun Government. After the war most of the large towns and ports in Sabah (North Borneo) were laid in ruins. All the efforts, and hardwork jointly shared by the people of Sabah, (North Borneo) and the Chartered Company Government in building up the country over the years into a peaceful and happy state, was destroyed. When the war was over, the army set up a military Administration in places recovered by battle. This included North Borneo, Labuan, Brunei and Sarawak. The British Borneo Civil Administration Unit governed under the direction of Major General Wootten, the Australian general officer in command, with headquarters at Labuan. The initials B.B.C.A.U. were spoken as one word Bu-Beekau, which came easily to the lips of all the people and helped to popularize that administration which carried on with much success.

Later, when two members of the British Parliament came out from London to North Borneo to report to Parliament on affairs in this distant part of the Commonwealth, they were surprised to learn from the Chiefs that the B.B.C.A.U. was the most popular form of Government they had yet experienced. Perhaps the issue of firearms to fight the few remaining Japanese was thought to be a feature of democracy, and made it popular.

On the declaration of armistic, the B.M.A. (British Military Administration) took over the whole of Sabah (British North Borneo). It was officially reported that the country was found to be in a state of appalling devastation. When the Australian Army returned, B.B.C.A.U. was succeeded by the British Military Administration (British North Borneo) known as B.M.A. This in turn was handed over to the Civil Government on the 15th July, 1946, with full ceremony at Kota Kinabalu (Jesselton).

The Chartered Company had agreed three weeks earlier with His Majesty's Secretary of State for the Colonies in London to cede to the Crown the territory known officially as the State of North Borneo, and thus with the addition of the island of Labuan to it, the new Colony of North Borneo came into being. Mr. James Calder an officer of the Malayan Civil Service assumed office as Acting Governor pending the appointment of Mr. E.F. (later Sir Edward), Twining, the first Governor of the new Colony. Sabah in 1946 was in ruins, and the first few years in the story of Sabah (North Borneo) as a British Crown Colony were ones of difficult struggle. Many experienced Government officers and Managers of Commercial firms had been killed by the Japanese or medically handicapped during the war. Most of the junior Asian staff had also perished.

There was no public utility services. Schools and Hospitals were non-existent. Disease and malnutrition were prevalent. Crime was rampant. Communications were practically non-existent. Food was scarce. The whole process of Government had come to a standstill as most of the Government records had been destroyed by the Japanese.

The Colony Government started to work to bring Sabah (North Borneo) back to a State of law and order. They obtained food for the people, started to rebuild houses, shops,

A monument put up at the surrender point Labuan Island, on the 9th September, 1945 to mark the location where the 32nd Japanese Southern Army in North Borneo and Sarawak surrendered.

2nd WORLD WAR
PEACE MONUMENT AT LABUAN, SABAH

This memorial is erected by the Japanese South Pacific Friendship Association in September, 1976 to preserve the memories of all soldiers, who fought and fell on this Island during the 2nd World War, and the memories of all civilian who perished with them. May it stand a lasting monument of human courage and devotion to duty and may it symbolise the fervent desire of every man, woman and child on this Island that never again wll this Island be a witness to so much suffering and miseries.

*The Australian World War
Two Memorial at Labuan Island
British North Borneo (Sabah)*

*War Graves of the
Fallen Australian
Heroes of World
War II at Labuan
Island*

The Indian Infantry war memorial at Labuan Island

schools, Hospitals, etc. Crimes were stopped and did what they could to repair the roads, bridges and the railways.

The trade of Sabah had to be started again. The rubber estates and timber camps had to be opened up once more and the Government had to start working again.

By the end of 1947 once again Sabah (North Borneo) was selling timber and rubber to the outside world. Food was being brought in sufficient for the people. Many visitors had come to see if they could plant new crops such as cocoa, and oil palm and re-start tobacco planting on Estates.

By the end of 1947 Sabah had a favourable trade. This favourable trade balance continued in 1948. In 1950 to 1951 the amount of trade balance has greatly improved and increased, due to the great demand for more rubber during the Korean War. By 1952 plans for the re-building of towns were ready and work started. Slowly and steadily, the new towns grew up.

Colonial rule came to an end on midnight the 15th September, 1963 but before that, on the 31st August, 1963 Sabah had been given self-government under its own Chief Minister and Ministers. For a brief period, Sabah was an independent nation.

The Governor of the Colony of North Borneo, Sir William Goode handed over power to the State Legislative Assembly under its Chief Minister. On the evening of the 16th September 1963, the Governor, Sir William Goode, stepped on board H.M.S. Lion shortly afterwards the ship pulled away from the Kota Kinabalu (Jesselton) wharf, while retiring British officials and newly independent Sabah State leaders stood at the salute. It was a very impressive and historical farewell. The people of Sabah became independent, masters of their fate and members of a new nation, as the thirteenth States of Malaysia.

Farewell Parade In Honour Of His Excellency, Sir William Goode, at Kota Kinabalu Wharf, Sabah, the last British Governor to leave the colony of North Borneo on the 16th Sept 1963. By H.M.S. Lion

8

What the People Say About the Japanese

Datuk J.R. Baxter
PGDK, CBE., JP.
Retired Estate Manager
Sapong, Tenom.

My first meeting with the Japanese was after they had taken over North Borneo, as it was then, a Japanese Officer and four regular soldiers came up to Sapong Estate, where I was staying and working as a Manager.

The only awkward moment was when going round with the Japanese Officer, we came on the burnt smoke houses where I had burnt all the rubber under instructions from Jesselton (as Kota Kinabalu was known then), but he did not hit me.

The officer and soldiers behaved well. We all had lunch together before the officers left for Beaufort, and after he had left the soldiers asked if they could have four bottles of my beer. I told them we would cause no trouble, so long as they did not interfere with woman in any way.

The Tenom District Officer, John Marcatney was brought over from Tenom and he, I and my three European Assistants were put in one room and the door nailed shut.

In the morning, we were let out and thanked for not trying to escape. The Japanese Officer came back and we were told to go to Tenom Lama, the old Railway Station, and proceeded to walk there carrying what we could in the way of clothes.

The Japanese officer caught up with us riding in my car and we were told to get in, but I said we would walk, but were then told in no uncertain terms to get in, which we did. The officer and regular soldiers behaved well, no complaints, we went to Jesselton by train.

Arriving in Jesselton, where all the Europeans were housed in a School, very crammed but were treated, reasonably well. After some weeks, we were then shipped to Kuching, Sarawak, via Labuan, all living in the hold alongside each other, very crammed.

Arrived in Kuching, we were all housed in the Prisoners of War Camp, with temporary buildings, and at first were reasonably treated, going out morning and afternoon to plant vegetables for our own consumption, but when the war started to go against the Japanese, very different marched out morning and afternoon under guard to plant crops for the Japanese, but I was lucky for sometime as I and two other looked after 50 pigs for the Japanese, collecting from all camp kitchens, what was thrown away and cooking it up in a big oil drums. One interesting thing happened, a pig from a Chinese Towkay started coming around the styes, so we gradually gave it food until we got it to come into an empty stye, where Sam Chisholm, a New Zealander, killed it with an axe. I cut it up into small pieces and put them into two tongs, put sacking on the top and pig manure on top of that, when we were carrying the two tongs back to the camp we met an officer, put down the tongs and bowed as we had to. He said what are you carrying? We said manure for our garden of vegetables, so had the only pork chop that night during my 3½ years in Kuching.

We always had to bow when meeting a Japanese and early on was slapped not badly, for not bowing, so unlike the Prisoners of War, who were beaten up for not doing anything they were supposed to.

We had no clothes to speak of, and I just wore a pair of shorts, originaly two, but as they wore out made one pair sticking the parts together with latex, always bare feet no shoes.

The Prisoners of War just wore a G. string. I went in at 13 stone and came out at 8 stone, while P.O.Ws were dying at 10 a day towards the end and always given a military funeral, at any time the Japanese did nothing for them. The guards were Koreans under Japanese Officers & N.C.Os and were also beaten up if they did anything wrong. The treatment of the Priosners of War was shocking, beaten up daily and starved.

The English Officers had a seperate camp and were treated better. There were camps for Prisoners of War Officers, Women, our camp and one camp for Priests.

As an example of how we were treated was that in 3 1/2 years we had one Red Cross parcel divided among 6 while when the Australians came in there was a Godown full of Red Cross parcels.

In our camp we lost about 10% of weight through lack of food, while for the P.O.Ws it must have been over 50%. They were walking skeletons, no back side, where their spine ended their legs started. I and Datuk Robert Evan's father Dick Evans, Resident, Jesselton, were taken round the hospital when the Australians came in and saw these skeletons lying on beds and we told nothing could be done for them, whatever they were given just went straight through them.

I do not think Major Suga in charge of the Camp was a bad man, but had to act under orders. He cut his throat when the Australians came in, while the Japanese Officers, bastards without exception, were taken by the Australians to Labuan and shot, nothing much that I have read, has been written about this Japanese Kuching Prisoners of War camp. A few of the worst Koreans just disappeared after the Australians came in and think probably some of the released prisoners of war were responsible.

When we killed the Chinese pig, we sent a note to the Towkay, we will pay you when the war ends and got a reply never mind paying I will try and send another.

I and Datuk Robert Evan's father, Dick Evans, Resident Kota Kinabalu, (Jesselton) slept next to each other and shared everything, while in Kuching, but two on my other side died, Bidmead an engineer, and the other, a Government Officer, Cole Adams, died the day after the Australians came in. His father was in charge of the North Borneo Police.

Finally, an example of the condition of the Prisoners of War I was on a survey party measuring the camps and our measurement chain went across the hut of one of the P.O.W. skeleton sitting in a drain, he made no movements whatsoever and was dead, I think in a day or two ago.

Datuk J.R. Baxter, PGDK. JP, CBE

Tuan Haji Zainal Bin Awang Damit Pensioner-Marine Department North Borneo (Sabah)

Tuan Haji Zainal Bin Awang Damit
Chief Clerk
Marine Department, Sabah
Pensioner (May, 1969)
Kg. Batu Arang,
Labuan.

During the Japanese occupation in North Borneo (Sabah), I was working as a Clerk, attached to the District Office Labuan, under a Japanese officer.

I still remembered that on the 6th September, 1942, forty-eight years ago today, the Japanese Government ordered the people of Labuan to be assembled at the Labuan Airfield, to welcome the arrival of General Maidato Commander-in-Chief of the wartime Japanese Armed Forces in British Borneo, who flew from Sibu, Sarawak, to Labuan to declare the new Japanese Airfield opened.

A large crowd of people including myself, were waiting at the Labuan Airfield, these were Government Servants, Towkays, Teachers, School-Children, Village Headmen, etc. The crowd numbered more than a thousand people.

We all waited for several hours at the Airfield, until 3.00 p.m. but there was no sign, whatsoever, of any aircraft coming. The Japanese officer gave orders that the crowd may disperse for a while, and take shelters nearby until they were ordered to re-assemble in their respective places in the Airfield. The sun was very bright and it was very hot that day.

The people waited for a long time, until late evening. The aircraft never came. Finally the Japanese officer announced that the General will not be coming to Labuan, and gave orders that all those present at the Airfield, may go home. After the announcement, all the Japanese officers left, including the people.

Few weeks later we received news that General Maida was killed in an aircraft accident. The plane carrying General Maida with other Japanese officers crashed at Bintulu, Sarawak, killing all its occupants.

On the 9th day of September, 1942 Labuan Island was named "Maida Island", by the Japanese Government. The memorial was made by order of General Tojo and was officially declared opened by General Tojo himself who passed through Labuan Island in July, 1945.

Unquote.

The plaque read as follows:-

"This Memorial Commemorates General Maida, Commander-in-Chief of the wartime Japanese Forces in British Borneo who was killed in an aircrash at Bintulu, on 6th September, 1942 when en-route to Labuan to open the Airfield here. On 9th December,

1942 Labuan was named Maida Island by the Japanese Government. The Memorial was made by order of General Tojo, who passed through Labuan in July, 1945."

Any visitors to Labuan Island, may have a look at the Memorial, which was located in front of the District Office, Labuan. Tuan Haji Zainal Bin Awang Damit's memory is still fresh, when the Japanese re-named Labuan, to Maidato Island. He retired from the Marine Department, Sabah, in May 1969 and is currently residing at Kg. Batu Arang, Labuan.

MUNJONG BIN YAHYA
RETIRED CUSTOMS OFFICER
SANDAKAN
(Source : "Still Serving" Vol. 1 December, 1970 Magazine)

In 1938 I joined the North Borneo Volunteer Force, and in 1939 I left for Singapore with the intention of joining the Malay Regiment, but was unable to do so for various reasons. When the Japanese invaded Malaya (West Malaysia), I enlisted as an Air Raid Warden with the Bukit Timah Road Unit, Singapore, and carried out my duties until the fall of Singapore, on the 15th February, 1942. In 1944, by order of the Japanese Military to return to Sandakan (North Borneo) in a small boat, I was kept in a batch. It took us almost a month to reach Sandakan.

While at Labuan, one of my former volunteer colleague (Sergeant Patrick Jup) asked me about the war situation and I told him that there was every chance for the Allies to return soon. Because there were lot of spies working for the Japanese, we had to seperate quickly. Early 1945, I was employed as a Boatman by the Japanese, and ordered to proceed to Jambangan Island. On board were two Japanese Military Police – "Kempeitai".

The purpose of the visit was to investigate into the report that the people on the Island were against the Japanese.

We did not go to the Island, instead went direct to Musar Island.

I knew that one of the Towkays in one of the shops had weapons. Early in the morning when we reached the jetty, I asked one of my companions to see the Towkay (Shop Proprietor) and to seek assistance from him to kill the two Japanese "Kempeitai".

As we were approaching the shop, suddenly shots rang out from the direction of the shops and killed the two Japanese. The Towkay was no other than Tuan Haji Abu Bakar Tan Teck Bak (Now Tuan Haji Datuk Abu Bakar Tan) who is a prominent business man.

I stayed with them for quite sometime before I joined the Guerrillas organised by the Australian Army on Jambangan Island. After two month's training I and my colleagues were sent to Sugut, at Pomotudun, where we killed eleven Japanese in the house.

We were under the command of Colonel Chester. My unit operated in the jungle until the Japanese surrendered. After the war, I was awarded the Victory Medal, the King's Medal, the War Medal and the Pacific Star.

Datuk Haji Abu Bakar Tan, AMN, PGDK.
Sandakan, Sabah.
(Source : "Still Serving" Vol. 1 December, 1970 Magazine)

During the Second World War, I was purely a merchant at a small Island called Musa near Kudat. After the Japanese invasion in 1941, the whole of South Pacific was occupied by the Japanese Army, including Sabah (British North Borneo).

At that time the Chairman of the Chinese Chamber of Commerce Mr. Chang Su Yin and Mr. Ho See, who was a member of the North Borneo Volunteer Force were forced to escape and they took refuge at my place, unfortunately the Japanese collaborators came to know about this and made a report to the Japanese Military Police (Kempeitai) who immediately set out by boat to arrest these group of people.

Fortunately, I came to know about this and I assisted them to escape before the Japanese arrived. When the Japanese arrived, they threatened me to tell them where these group of people were hiding, otherwise my whole family and relatives would be executed. They also accused me of being anti-Japanese.

I was tortured cruely and most inhumanly, twice, by the Japanese. As a result of this tortures, my body was full of bruises and scars. Because of Justice and my strong spirit of self-sacrifice, I was prepared to die in order to save the lives of my friends.

After being tortured by the Japanese, the Kempeitai wanted to take me away to Kudat for execution, but a group of six courageous friends of mine, Ng Kim See, Marilan, Mongukap, Abdullah and Kamang, decided with strong determination, that they would prefer to die together for the sake of freedom and justice and attacked the Japanese and killed two Japanese Military Police (Kempeitais) and two collaborators. Following the attack, they captured from the Japanese, two rifles, two revolvers, few dozen hand-granades, few dozen smoke-screen bombs and few hundred rounds of ammunition.

We started a guerrilla groups, and because of knowing the places so well, we easily won the support of the local people who gladly joined us.

Before long, I sailed in a small boat to Tawi Tawi, Southern Philippines, and made a report to Colonel Suarez of the United States Philippines Guerrilla Headquarters, who then sent a cable to United Kingdom for help. Immediately United Kingdom Government sent out Major Chester, with another British officer and an Australian radio operator with another Australian born Chinese called Wong Yee Choy, to Musa Island in a submarine. The leader of our guerrilla was Tun Datu Haji Mustapha Bin Datu Harun. I was then a Section Leader, S.R.A. We captured large quantity of arms and ammunitions and used these captured arms to fight against the Japanese and killed many of them.

After the war, I was awarded by the King of Great Britain a King's Medal for Bravery, the 1939-1945 War Medal and the Pacific Star. When the war was over, I returned to my home town and started my own business again, trading as Thai Hong Hong, dealing with Imports and Exports. It is reliably learned that Datuk Haji Abu Bakar Tan is currently living with his son in Vancouver, Canada.

Mr. Paddy H. Funk (Deceased)
Sandakan, Sabah.
(The Late Paddy H. Funk was a representative of North Borneo Volunteer guerrillas in the Great Victory Celebrations held in London on 8th June, 1946).
(Source : "Still Serving" Vol. 1 December, 1970 Magazine)

This is a true story of my experience during World War II. We were three brothers (Sandakanites) who were captured by the Japanese Kempeitai in 1943 for being members of the underground which assisted Australian soldiers in captivity. We were brutally tortured and imprisoned for years and our brother, Alexander, was executed with eight others including an Australian Army Captain L.C. Mathews, of the 8th Division, Australian Imperial Forces.

We supplied food, medicine, radio parts, Japanese shipping and troop movements information to the Allies, and helped prisoners of war to escape to the Philippines.

It was dusk on 19th July, 1943 and I had just finished my mearge dinner of "Ubi Kayu" (Tapioca) when there was a "bang" at my front door followed by a kick. I knew there were coming for me, and my younger brother Alexander and a number of my friends had been taken away by them about a fortnight ago. From my window, I could see a truck load of Japanese soldiers fully armed with fixed bayonets waiting at the roadside. I unlocked the door and saw an officer of the dreaded Japanese Kempeitai with two burly soldiers.

Without warning, he gave me one big slap on my face followed by a kick to my stomach. He nodded to the two soldiers to take me to the waiting truck right away. I pleaded with the officer that I may be allowed to take some clothes along with me, this was refused. They even forbade me to say goodbye to my wife and two children who were crying at one corner of the house.

I was taken to the "House of Torture" that was the name we gave to the Japanese Military Police Headquarters at Sandakan. This building was the official residence of the General Manager of Bakau and Kenya Extract Company. The Japanese had turned this once beautiful bungalow into a Military Police Headquarters.

For one whole week I was left alone in a dark room below the building. I could hear the shouting, yelling, groaning and beating almost every day and night of my friends and the Australian Soldiers who were interrogated by the Japanese Military officers.

After one week, they took me upstairs to join the rest of the people who were arrested in connection with the case. There were more than 100 of us in that big room, and these were Japanese guards all around us with fixed bayonets. No one was allowed to talk, smile or even look at each other; except to look down at the floor in front of you, where we were all made to sit down crosslegged.

Anyone found smiling was mercilessly beaten up by at least three to four guards. These guards really enjoyed beating us. My eldest brother John was there and so was my younger brother Alexander. My brother Alexander, Sergeant Abing of the North Borneo Armed Constabulary and myself used to meet Captain L.C. Mathews, under a huge three in the jungle which is next to my father's rubber estate at mile 7½ adjacent to mile 8 Government Agricultural Experimental Station of which a Police Station was specially constructed as a look-out post for any escape of POWs for mile 8 1/4 camp under the charge of Sergeant Abing. Three of us met Captain Mathews several times and on one occasion, my brother Alex gave Captain Mathews a .38 revolver which he had secretly taken from the North Borneo Volunteer Force Armoury two days before the landing of the Japanese Shock Troops. He even had his .303 rifle buried at our rubber estate at Mile 7½ just adjacent to "B" Force Camp; instead of surrendering it to the North Borneo Volunteer Force Armourer as instructed by our Commanding Officer, Captain H. Parvell.

When the Japanese found this out through the betrayal of one of the locals, they brutally tortured him and hung him upside down. Every part of his body was swollen. They brought Alex to the rubber estate and forced him to dig up the hidden rifle which was in good condition. My brother John and myself were again tortured and beaten up with wooden swords as the Japanese strongly suspected that we must have buried our rifles somewhere in the estates, as well.

The Japanese Kempeitai and the burley guards hated us very much because the three of us, brothers, committed the same offence against them.

The officers said they had witnesses involved in the case, who were willing to testify against us that the three of us had threatened and forced them to help the prisoner of war or else reprisals would be taken against them when the British returned.

We were subjected to the disbolic water torture (filled with water and rice) then the Japanese guards step on our swollen stomachs, the Bakau firewood torture, burnt with fag ends, whipped and bashed, but we did not give in.

On October 25th 1943, the Japanese took 53 of us (the rest were released), from all walks of life, doctor, dental-surgeon, traders, towkays, police inspector, sergeants, policemen, Jemadar detectives, clerks, forest-ranger, overseers, watchman, boatmen and labourers, comprising of multi-racial group of people, Europeans, Eurasian, Chinese, Dusuns/Kadazans, Sikh, Muruts, Suluks, Filipinos, Javanese and Mrs. M.Y. Cohen, a wealthy Jewess woman, together with 19 Australian Prisoner-of-war and 5 European civilians and their wives, who were involved in the "Sandakan underground movements".

We were shipped like cattle in a small coastal boat to Kuching, Sarawak, and imprisoned in the "Torture Prison" a military prison for final judgement to be passed on us by high-ranking Japanese Military officers. This prison was specially reconstructed for mental tortures. There were 12 wire cages approximately the size of a small room measuring 20 ft wide x 20 ft long x 7 ft high, and 25 men were squeezed into a cage and were made to sit inside crosslegged. We stayed in these cages from October, 1943 to July 1944.

After the month in the "Mental Torture Prison" the Japanese fined the following towkays of Sandakan, heavily before they (my fellow prisoners) were released: –

Mrs. M.Y. Cohen, Mr. Khoo Siak Chew (Former Minister of Communication and Works, Sabah) Mr. Lo Hoi Chee (Manager, Gambling Syndicate), Mr. Wong Wee Man (Manager, King's theatre) Mr. Kwan Chu Ming of Kwong Borneo Development and Mr. Kwan Ming Ming also of Kwong Borneo Development.

On March 1st 1944 John and myself were sentenced to nine years military imprisonment and my younger brother Alexander together with seven others were sentenced to death.

The eight condemned were shot by a Japanese firing squad on a hot noon on 2nd March, 1944 together with the gallant Australian Captain L.C. Mathews, M.C., of the 8th Division, Australian Imperial Forces, who was posthumously awarded the George Cross in March, 1944. This brave Captain could have easily escaped, because we wanted to be in the Philippines so that he could negotiate for guns and ammunitions to arm the 2,750 Allied soldiers in the POW camp.

He told us that his duty was to stand by with his boys and that he must go through thick and their with them under any circumstances. So instead we contacted Wong Muk Sing, a Chinese-Filipino guerrila to get arms. This barter-trader who was introduced to me by Mr. Quadra, another Filipino guerrilla was one of those executed by the Japanese on 2nd March, 1944.

On 19th September 1945 we were liberated by the 7th Australian Division. On September 20th 1945 they sent us by air back to Labuan, where we were all looked after by the Australian 9th Division at the Convalescent Camp at Timbali, Labuan.

I was sent back to Sandakan on 25th November, 1945 after recovering from the Australian Red Cross Hospital, Labuan.

Unquote

Mr. Paddy H. Funk was also a founder member of the "United Peranakan Association Sabah". He died in Australia about a year ago.

9
Conclusion

The Japanese Army has 51 divisions of which 11 can be spared from duties in China, Indochina and at home to join the offensive against the Allies.

The Japanese Navy has 10 battleships, six large and four smaller carriers, 36 cruisers, 113 destroyers and 63 submarines. There is no independent air force but the Navy has about 1000 aircrafts, half of them carrier borne, which will be committed along with about half of the Army's 1500 planes.

It is clear that with such forces the Japanese cannot hope to win an all-out war against the United States and the British Empire. Instead their aim is to take advantage of the distraction provided by the war in Europe and seize the resource producing areas of Malaya and the East Indies.

They will then be self-sufficient and will hope to defend a fortified perimeter around their conquests so fiercely that Britain and the United States will make peace. As well as the economic and militaristic pressure supporting the plan, there is also an element of broader Asian Nationalism which sees value in the Asian Co-Prosperity Sphere which is to be created.

The attack on Pearl Harbour has been planned to disable the United States Navy for the time required for the creation of the defensive perimeter. Admiral Yamamoto, who commands the Japanese Combined Fleet and has been responsible for the planning of the attack, is however, deeply pessimistic about the eventual outcome.

He sees the Pearl Harbour success as illusory and as granting only six months respite before Japan is swamped by United States production. In greater detail the plan provides in the first phase for four divisions of Twenty-fifth Army to advance into Malaya (Malaysia) to take Singapore after landing in Thailand; for two divisions of Fifteenth Army to move into Burma from Thailand for two and a half divisions of Fourteenth Army to take the Philippines, and for other units to take Hong Kong, Guam, Wake and Makin Islands.

The second and subsequent phases will see the same forces being regrouped and moving onto Borneo, Sumatra and Java; the Bismarcks and New Guinea and into Burma in strength.

If one looks back to the history of Japan in the century leading to the Second World War, it can easily be seen that it advanced from a primitive, fuedal and isolated nation to a leading world military power.

It was able to do so by catching up with the rest of the world, particulary in the field of technology, by its extra ordinary ability to copy. People, customs and national characteristics, however, cannot change so rapidly, and the revolution in Japanese technology and military might was not accompanied by similarly revolutionary changes in its people.

I have reason to believe that the rapid rise to military power, far in advance of changes in attitudes, was the basic reason for the Japanese atrocities. The community of Nations took some centuries to evolve more humane attitudes in respect of behaviour in war then those obtained twenty centuries ago.

The Japanese, were not in step with other nations and as a result, the treatment of people in Japanese occupied territority and of prisoners of war, was much the same as that of centuries ago when conquerors brutalised the vanquished, made them slaves and regarded them as expendable.

The post-war rise of Japan as a world economic power is much different in character to its rise in military prowess, although it has been as surprising and rapid. Many countries are now dependent on its goodwill and on decisions made in Japan.

Japan today, at least outwardly, is undoubtedly a different Japan from that of 1941-1945. The revolution of Japan aimed at and introduced during the United States occupation under General MacArthur, has produced a more democratic Japan with many different outlooks and customs.

The modern Japanese are more westernised, and although their leaders and businessmen have certain ways and adopt certain attitudes not easily understood by us, they fit more comfortably into the international business community. They have been drastic fundamental changes to Japanese institutions and Japan has abandoned its isolation by moving to the front of the stage in the fields of world trade and financc.

The wartime actions and attitudes of so many different Japanese, seen in the context of prior Japanese history, could only have been based on some fundamental features in the structure of Japanese society and culture.

The Japanese people, at least originally, appeared to embrace the steps aimed at preventing Japan being led into another war. They had experienced the atomic bomb and otherwise had suffered greatly with an enormous number of soldiers and civilians killed and maimed. The appalling consequences of the war in its last year to the Japanese people, apart from the bomb, are not always appreciated. However, with the coming of new generations, memories fade and circumstances, including National feelings, change.

National interests change. In 1946 the concern of the United States was to prevent its former enemy, Japan from repeating its past actions. As the years passed, concerned about its former enemy has changed to concern about its former ally, as the United

States and USSR confront each other as super powers. The United States interest has now changed to have Japan ignore some of the constitutional prohibitions in respect of military capacity, in order to provide for its own defense and provide a buffer to USSR expansion into South Asia and the Pacific.

World War Two meant many things to many people. To over fifty million men, women, and children, it meant death. To hundreds of millions more in the occupied areas and theaters of combat, the war meant hell on earth. Many individuals gave their lives in the belief that they were sacrificing themselves for such ideals. At the same time, to most high officials the war meant, above all, Power Politics at its fiercest. It has long been observed that it is easier to begin wars than to end them. Let this be a lesson to all mankind. World War Two has indeed changed the face of the globe. Peace is the Best.

Chronology of World War II –
Borneo

7th December, 1941. (Pearl Harbour)

At 0755 Hawaiian time Japanese carrier aircraft attack the main base of the United States Pacific Fleet at Pearl Harbour. There is complete tactical and strategic surprise.

The Japanese have sent six carriers, Akagi, Kaga, Hiryu, Soryu Zuikaku and Shokaku, with a total of 423 planes embarked to make the attack. The pilots are brilliantly trained and their equipment is good. Admiral Nagumo commands and he has, in addition to the carriers, two battleship and two heavy cruisers in his force along with destroyers and other supporting vessels including tankers.

Two waves of attacks are sent in. Commander Fuchida leads the first strike with 40 tropedoo bombers (with special shallow running tropedoes) 51 dive bombers, 50 high-level bombers and 43 fighters.

The Second wave is of similar strength but with extra dive bombers replacing the tropedo aircraft. All eight US battleships in port are damaged, five of them sinking. (USS Arizona is a total loss; Oklahoma will be raised but scrapped; California, Naveda and West Virginia will be rebuilt and will rejoin the US fleet later in the war.) Three cruisers and three destroyers are also sank. The Americans lost 188 aircraft from the island's air-fields. The Japanese lost 29.

16/12/1941 (Borneo)

Early in the day there are Japanese landings at Miri, Seria and Lutong, State of Sarawak. The oil plants are set on fire before the small British and Dutch forces retreat. The Japanese force is from 16th Infantry Division and they have considerable naval support.

23/12/1941 (Borneo)

There are Japanese landings at Kuching, the capital of Sarawak. Two transports are sunk and two damaged by a Dutch submarine. A second submarine sinks a Japanese destoryer but is then sunk in turn. The small British forces at Kuching resists until 25th December, 1941 and then withdraws.

1/1/1942 (Borneo)

Sabah (North Borneo) was invaded by the Japanese, Labuan Island was taken.

2/1/1942

The Japanese invaded the mainland of Sabah (North Borneo) by way of Mempakul.

3/1/1942

The Japanese took Beaufort.

19/1/1942

The Japanese took Sandakan, the former state capital of Sabah (North Borneo).

9/10/1943

Kinabalu Guerrillas attacked the Japanese, on the eve of the Double Tenth, Chinese Festival.

19/12/1943

Lieutenant Albert Kwok – The North Borneo Guerrilla Chief surrended to the Japanese Military Authorities.

21/1/1944

Lieutenant Albert Kwok and his band of guerrillas were killed by the Japanese at Petagas. (A memorial garden was built on the spot where the execution was carried out.)

27-30/4/1945 (Borneo)

Admiral Barkey leads a squardon of three cruisers and six destroyers in a preparatory bombardment of targets in the Tarakan area in the Northeast of the Island.

On the 30th there is a small landing by a U.S. Force on the offshore Island of Sadan.

12/9/1945

18-20/6/1945 (Borneo)

In the North, Australian troops take Tutong (Brunei) on the 18th and on the 19th there are Australian landings at Mempakul. On the 20th there are landing at Lutong, Sarawak.

10/6/1945 (Borneo)

Almost 30,000 men of the 9th Australian Infantry Division land from a naval force commanded by Admiral Royal in Brunei Bay and on the Island of Labuan and Muara (Brunei) nearby.

A preparatory bombardment has been fired by a force of cruisers and destroyers under the command of Admiral Barkey.

13/6/1945 (Borneo)

United States and Australian troops enter Borneo Town.

25/6/1945 (Borneo)

In Sarawak the Australian forces complete the occupation of the Miri oilfield area.

1/7/1945 (Borneo)

After a preparatory bombardment beginning on 25th June by nine cruisers and 13 destroyers led by Admiral Barley, 33,000 men of the reinforced 7th Australian Division land at Balikpapan (Southern Borneo). Three escort carriers give support to the landings for the first three days ashore. General Milford commands the troops.

3/7/1945 (Borneo)

The troops landed at Balikpapan (Southern Borneo) take Sepinggan airfield and by 5th have cleared most of the oil producing area in the immediate vicinity.

12/7/1945 (Borneo)

There is an Allied landing at Andus. Australian troops take Maradi in the north of the Island.

9/9/1945

The 32nd Japanese Southern Army in North Borneo and Sarawak surrendered to the Allied Forces at Labuan.

The surrender of Japanese forces in South East Asia is concluded before Admiral Mountbaten in Singapore. The Japanese garrisons in the various islands of the Pacific and in East Indies will also surrender one by one in the next few days.

15/7/1946

State of North Borneo, (Sabah) became a British Crown Colony.

15/9/1963

Colonial Rule in North Borneo (Sabah) came to an end at midnight.

31/8/1963

Sabah achieved Independence through Malaysia (The 13th States of Malaysia)

16/9/1963

Sir William Goode left Sabah by H.M.S. Lion. He was the last Governor of Sabah.

APPENDIX II

BRITISH NORTH BORNEO HERALD –
17th OCTOBER 1940
– SPITFIRE FUND – LIST OF SUBSCRIBERS

THE

BRITISH NORTH BORNEO HERALD

AND

FORTNIGHTLY RECORD

NO. 20.—VOL. LVIII   SANDAKAN, THURSDAY, 17TH OCTUBER, 1940   Price 15 cts

CONTENTS

Spitfire Fund

Acknowledgments of the remittances that we have been able to make for the purchase of two "Spitfires" have been received from two sources. The British Broadcasting Corporation, in their broadcasts at 7.30 and 9.00 p.m. on the 28th of September and at 12.30 a.m. on the 29th mentioned the gift of a second Spitfire by the people of North Borneo and in addition His Excellency the Governor received the following telegram from Lord Beaverbrook, the Minister for Aircraft Production:—

"The continuing support given by the people of North Borneo to the Royal Air Force is a matter of the highest encouragement to all in Britain. We welcome this second generous gift as magnificent proof of the unselfish devotion of North Borneo to the cause of Freedom and Justice for which the Empire fights and as proof to the world of our indomitable determination to achieve victory. The name of North Borneo will shortly be written in triumph in the skies".

The Fund is still progressing and there are 190 units collected at the date of going to press, of which 170 units ($65,000) have already been remitted.

Progress is not as fast as could be wished, for we must remember that the aeroplanes are required as soon as they can be supplied. We cannot give too much or too quickly. Remember the old adage :—

For lack of a nail, a shoe was lost !
For lack of a shoe, a horse was lame !
For lack of a horse, a rider was late !
For lack of a rider, a battle was lost !
By losing a battle, a kingdom was lost !
And all for lack of a nail.

And it might well be that for the lack of a Spitfire that we might and could have supplied an air battle that could have been a glorious and decisive victory might be a defeat.

Subscriptions should be sent to the Treasurer, Spitfire Fund, c/o State Bank, Sandakan.

17th Oct., 1940   THE BRITISH NORTH BORNEO HERALD   279

North Borneo Spitfire Fund

First List of Subscribers

H. E. Mr. C. R. Smith	$2,000.00
Mr. and Mrs. McGechan	500.00
The Hon. Mr. G. L. Gray	500.00
J. B. Colman and Pitas Estate	400.00
The Hon. Mr. F. W. Pinnock	500.00
Customs and Marine Department	1,011.00
G. Mavor	500.00
Public Works Department Sandakan and Jesselton	2,000.00

FOREST AND AGRICULTURAL DEPARTMENTS.

Contributions of 80 cents each:

Abdul bin Toran, Abdullah, Ah Yin, Ah Yun, Bobo, Chin Kiaw, Chong Moi, Hoo Kaw, Junnis, Lee Moi, Liew Moi, Pun Moi, Rais, Sei Moi, Sarjo bin Sariman, To Moi (16) $12.80

Contributions of $1.00 each:

Abdul Hamid bin Md. Daud, Ah Wing bin Chaka, Ali, Allen, Billy, Audu bin Patrick, Arumpad bin Manggong, Atek bin Kiduagan, Ayus bin Arjau, Bongso bin Abdullah, P. Escobar, Gujing bin Iga, Gusti Salinan bin Gusti Ismail, Hassan bin Brahim, Hussin bin Amat, Ibrahim bin Walli, Ismail bin A. Rahman, Kalibus bin Guojun, Kumis bin Chabang, Kassim bin Tongon, Kinin bin Sambaing, G. Labuan, Limau bin Sarang, Madun bin Duraman, Mael bin Mohamad, Majuyap bin Majuni, Mikal bin Matasan, Mohamed bin Kula, Naun bin Mutu, Onggib bin Suak, Osip bin Kelito, Babayoi bin Silak, Sabiah bin Amboli, Sahari bin Idris, Salamat bin Tumit, Salleh bin Amit, Samak bin Manggoug, Sitau bin Kiwing, Sunggin bin Bungkalat (38)   38.00

Contributions of 50 cents each:

Peling bin Atin, Sitta, Sikajat bin Buhanji, Tinggal, Umbol bin Duuya, Dawai bin Dipal, Dippal bin Lantid, Gapar, Kadir bin Abdul, Laiman, Abdul Hamid bin Mustapha, Ahmad, Amit, Augustine (14)   7.00

Contributions of $3.00 each:

Abdul Kahar bin Abdullah, Chu Kui You (2)   6.00

Contributions of $1.50 each:

Abdullah bin Suping, Lee Koh Huat, Masi, Noordin bin Tumbi (4)   6.00

J. Agama   30.00

Contributions of $1.20 each:

Ah Fook, Bain, Esmael, Hiew Kian, Mataail, Ng Sam Kan, Otto, Stassins bin Raymon, Tahir, Taria (10)   12.00

Contributions of $1.60 each:

Ah Mat, Chan Yiu Sang, Chou Soo Hoi, Chin Kong (4)   6.40

Contributions of $15.00 each:

Ali bin Penilek, F. M. Calacala, D. V. Fermin (3)   45.00

Contributions of 30 cents each:

Amat Kriya, Tai Mah (2)   .60

Contributions of 75 cents each:

Amat bin H. Brahim, Yusop bin Ali (2)   1.50

Contributions of $25.00 each:

L. Apostol, A. Colludo, W. G. Higgins, F. Melogrito (4)   100.00

Contributions of 20 cents each:

Arsat, Chong Ah Quen, J. Lo, Madusiu (4)   .80

Contributions of 40 cents each:

Asaan, M. Chung, J. Garcia, Jappar, Kassiin, Liaw Sau, Messi, Tung Kiaw (8)   3.20

Contributions of 25 cents each:

Awang, Jumau bin Gimang, Matzin, Udin (4)   1.00

Carried forward $7,511.00

Brought forward		**$7,511.00**
Contributions of $2.00 each :		
Awang bin Rahman, Goh Ping Kun, Kou Abdullah bin Abdul Siddik, Lupang bin Tingkulus, Mail bin Alibo, Nawawi bin Abdul Latif, Harvey Siddik, Suleiman bin Latip, Tundum bin Sambas (9)	$18.00	
Ayaw	1.70	
Contributions of $20.00 each :		
D. Balajudin, M. Udarbe, H. King (3:	60.00	
Piah	1.40	
Kong Hoi Nin	6.00	
Kuen Tai	.65	
G. S. Brown	75.00	
Contributions of 60 cents each :		
Bongknng bin Kundiom, Tong Chin Miaw (2)	1.20	
Contributions of $5.00 each :		
P. Gastro, Wong Laun Fuk (2)	10.00	
Chau Kwai Shung	13.00	
Contributions of $10.00 each :		
Chaw Ah Lin, P. C. Clemente, J. A. Leano, J. Valera (4)	40.00	
Contributions of 55 cents each :		
Chou Chaw, Otto bin Amil (2)	1.10	
Choong Sau	.90	
Contributions of 35 cents each :		
Chin Moi, Yapp Siow (2)	.70	
H. G. Keith	100.00	
Contributions of $1.10 each :		
Kinta, Lee Sau, Liaw San, Mah Sau, Siaw San (5)	5.50	
J. T. Mudrana	7.50	
Contributions of 70 cents each :		
Saidau, Thien Koin (2)	1.40	
Contributions of $4.00 each :		
Puasa bin Sitam, Md., Wong Yun Siow (2)	8.00	622.35
The Hon. Mr. C. F. C. Macaskie	500.00	
Sandakan Lawn Tennis Club	500.00	
J. E. Longfield	500.00	
Mrs. J. E. Longfield	500.00	
Sandakan Club	500.00	
T. Efford	500.00	
Sabah Steamship Company, Limited	1,000.00	
Sandakan Dispensary, Limited	500.00	
Harrisons & Crosfield (B), Limited	1,000.00	
do. Subordinate Staff	500.00	
Mr. and Mrs. C. Boyer	500.00	
Secretariat Staff	500.00	
Messrs. Man Woo Loong	1,000.00	
Messrs. Kwan Shun Wing Company	500.00	
Messrs. Lo Pak Kat	500.00	
Contributions of $250.00 each :		
Messrs. Shing Kee, Hon. Mr. Kwan Yun Hin, Kwan Lok Ming, Messrs. Yung Soon, Poh Teck (5)	1,250.00	
Contributions of $150.00 each :		
Liau Kum Kee, Seow Siew Jitt (2)	300.00	
Contributions of $100.00 each :		
Wong Man Pun, Thomas Chan, Tong Watt, Messrs. Chip Luong (4)	400.00	
Contributions of $50.00 each :		
Yau Loo, Heng Wah, Soon Seng, Lai Piang Kee, Tai Loong, Luen Wah, Pun Too Heng, Kwong Teo Hing, Dr. C. T. Chan, Geor. Thien Man (10)	500.00	
Carried forward		$17,133.35

B ught forward		$17,133.35
Contributions of $25.00 each :		
John Funk, Chan Tian Joo, Kan Hing Lung (3)	$75.00	
Contributions of $20.00 each :		
Chin Guan, Hip Woo, Foo Wah, Chen Tung Chuan, Tin Sang, Kwong Yick Loon, Kwong Chuor , Soo Pat Kee, Heng Nyiap, Tai Cheong, Wai Woo Loong, Kian Ann, Su Kee Lau, Chuan Yick Lip, Chan Kam Man, Kwan Yick Club (16)	320.00	
Messrs. Yong Kee (Cheong Shu Fun)	30.00	
Contributions of $10.00 each :		
Soon Heng, Chin Hin, Chai Kee, Ng Kwok Choong Bus, Dr. Lau Chu Hsiah, Lau Thye Hon, Choong Kui Heong, Fong Choong Seng, Choong Hing, Guan Hong, Mau Sang, Meng Hing (12)	120.00	
Anthony Low	5.00	3,000.00
Lo Hoi Chee	25.00	
Kui Hin Club	15.40	
Kai Choo School children	11.60	
Contributions of $10.00 each :		
Ho Chan Woo, Lueng Shi Wing, Guan Hing, Wing Kwong, Tam Wing Kien, Lai Sing Lau, Tung Oan Association (7)	70.00	
Messrs. Funk and Sons	17.00	
Contributions of $5.00 each :		
Liau Wo Wai, Wah Fong, Chan Kee Yong, Sang Cheong, Yee Fung, Yong Chiap Joo, Sai Ho, Soon Heng (Bar), Yick Hong, Hien Woo Loong, Kwong Luen Shing, Cham Koon Yau, Hup Hin, San Pui Lai, Wing Sung Cheung, Man Cheong Lee, General Trading, Chee Cheong Shing, Kwan Ping Kwan, Lai Kam Wing, Man Fatt Hong, Sam Loong, Tai Kwong, Chung Man Hing, Hap Seng Lung, Siug Song, Chia Kon Shing, Tau Chung Kee, Loung Yick Chan, Lawrence Ho Tung, Yuen Woo Loong, Nam Thye, Lian Thye, Wong Wai Man, Wong Mun Wah, Hiong Kwong, Kong Chiu Association, Sui Chong, Hap Kee, Long Soon Heng, Lam Wing Hing, Kwong Hing Lung, Sin Cho Tong, Poh Wah, China Products Company (45)	225.00	
Contributions of $3.00 each :		
Guan Guan, Sui Sing, Cheng Tin, Pion Yick Sam, An Kin Lung (5)	15.00	
Contributions of $20.00 each :		
Teo Keon Association, Chong Mui (2)	40.00	
Meng Sin School children	15.93	
Keng Kiew Club	4.00	
Chung Wah School children	3.60	
Anonymous	3.37	
Contributions of $2.00 each :		
Lau and Koh, Yap Hen Moo, Hak Soon Club, Sam Kwong, Tan Ngoh, Hien Choon Lim, Yong Hnuh Seng, Hock Teo Huat, Hook Chiang, Ban Chuan Wie, Wong Suet Hap, Kwong Thye, Kuan Yick, Kien Chong, Wan Kee, Wing Hin Lung, Ku Man Chap, Tai Tung, Choo Ming, Wing Shum, Chiug Loo, Hinp Hing (22)	44.00	
Contributions of $1.00 each :		
San Kwok Min, Wai Sun, Tai Toh, Wong Fong Kee, Soon Sang Choong, Koo Sam Chua, Wing Cheong Lung, Man Woo, Yot Sang (9)	9.00	
Hang Fook Lung	1.50	600.00
Mrs. H. G. Keith		500.00
Dr. J. P. Curlile		500.00
J. K. S. Malcolm		500.00
Personnel of s.s. "Kinabalu"		500.00
G. Robertson		500.00
Dr. and Mrs. Tregarthen		500.00
Harrisons & Crosfield (B), Limited., Jesselton staff		500.00
	Carried forward	$24,133.35

Brought forward		$24,133.35
Jesselton Gymkhana Club		500.00
Anonymous		500.00
Hon. Mr. R. F. Evans		500.00
Rubber Restriction Department		500.00

WEST COAST PLANTERS ASSOCIATION

TUARAN AND TENGHILAN ESTATES

H. A. Byron	$500.00
I. R. H. Miller	116.81
Bernard Math	50.00
Fabian Soon	20.00
Tsen Shau Shong	15.00
Chung Ah Teck	10.00
John Barnard	12.00
Wong Yung	25.00
Chops Kian Chuan and Kian Hin	35.00
Labour Force and others	319.19

MELALAP ESTATE.

H. D. Lack	500.00
R. Mathews	150.00
D. P. Williams	50.00
Subordinate staff	50.00
W.C. Collard	500.00

LINGKUNGAN ESTATE.

Estate	1,714.00
Subordinate staff and labour force	180.00
F. H. Wrenn	600.00

BANGAWAN ESTATE.

Bangawan Estate	2,000.00
Cheah Loon Ghee & Co.	1,000.00
Sapong Estate—European Staff	1,500.00

LUMADAN ESTATE

J. S. McLaren	1,000.00
J. C. McGilvray	150.00
A. S. Simpson	150.00
Subordinate staff	200.00
Swee Hin	50.00
Sung Hou	50.00
Leong Song	25.00
J. A. Tayler	250.00

PADAS VALLEY ESTATE.

M. R. F. Lingard	500.00
J. J. Wilson	150.00
Benedict	60.00
Chau Poh An	50.00
Chop Wah Guan Chan	50.00
Ho Ah Lok	20.00
Ah Fatt	20.00
Ng Lu	15.00
Chong Pau	10.00
Subordinate staff and others	125.00

BEAUFORT ESTATE.

| Manager and Subordinate staff | 500.00 |

MENGGATAL ESTATE | 1,000.00 |

KIMANIS RUBBER LIMITED

W. Riddel	500.00
Mrs. Riddel	500.00
E. I. Morris	500.00
J. Elliott	500.00
R. J. C. Dobbie	500.00
R. B. Lutter	500.00
B. Falconer	500.00
Messrs. Chong Mun	50.00
Messrs. Man Foo	50.00
Messrs. Yeo Hin	50.00
Ng Wai Kwong	20.00

SUBORDINATE STAFF AND EMPLOYEES

| Kimanis Estate | 153.00 |
| Papar Estate | 100.00 |

Carried forward		$26,133.35

	Brought forward	$26,133.35
Mawao Estate	$75.00	
William Wong	25.00	
Noor Mohamed	25.00	
Kwong Hong Loong	25.00	

KINABUT ESTATE.

Mr. and Mrs. R. F. Jones	759.25	
Messrs. Au Yuk Mun	10.00	
Employees etc.	80.75	

WOODFORD ESTATE.

J. S. Morris	514.28	
Mrs. J. S. Morris	42.86	
Employees etc.	234.60	
Mandahan Estate Employees	50.00	

MEMBAKUT ESTATE.

P. F. Palmer	1,088.75	
Yan Wo Son	100.00	
Kalia Khan	100.00	
S. Tiong Bee	50.00	
Alam Khan	50.00	
S. Yun Loi	25.00	
S. Kok Teow	10.00	
Labour force and others	76.25	
		21,092.74
Tay Bee Chuan		500.00
Lands and Survey Department		500.00
Per Assistant District Officer, Tuaran		500.00
G. C. Fenton		500.00
Hon. Lt. Col. and Mrs. W. C. Adams		500.00
Chinese Advisory Board (Dr. Lau Lai, Mrs. Lee Chi On, Tay Bee Chuan, Oh Haw Teck, Lim Kong Sou, Chow Ah Qui)		500.00
J. C. Hood		500.00
Segama Estate		3,500.00
Government Staff, Tawau		500.00
H. E. Hopkins		500.00
Hon. Capt. and Mrs. W. A. C. Smolt		500.00
Treasury and State Bank Staff		1,000.00

MEDICAL DEPARTMENT.

Hon. Dr. J. P. Taylor	650.00	
Dr. M. C. Clarke	500.00	
Dr. K. H. Blaauw	480.00	
Miss M. North	178.57	
Dr. A. F. Stookes	115.00	
Miss E. Ashworth	100.00	
Chin Tin On	70.00	
Miss Winifred Chan	42.50	

Contributions of $30.00 each :

K. C. Liew, Chu Ah Loi (2)	60.00	

Contributions of $25.00 each :

Dr. K. Yamomoto, Thomas Chung Bou Hiau, Mohamed Yusoph bin Samsudin (3)	75.00	

Contributions of $20.00 each :

Paug Vui Chan, Miss Maxima Padama (2)	40.00	
A. E. Kong	19.00	

Contributions of $15.00 each :

Wong Bou Choon, Liew Yun Fatt, Cheah Sinn Sang, Stephen Pritchard (4)	60.00	

Contributions of $14.00 each :

Lae Thau Seng, Koh Yoo Loo (2)	28.00	
Lajian bin Cu	12.00	

Contributions of $10.00 each :

Kong Su En, Mrs. Mohd. Yusoph, Miss Norah Saiarda, Miss Alice Watson, Chin Yun Eu, Liew Kim Shing, Mohamed Gani, Miss Matilda Collado (8)	80.00	

Contributions of $8.00 each :

Richard Low, Steenie Chung (2)	16.00	

(To be continued in the next issue) $50,726.09

APPENDIX III
BRITISH NORTH BORNEO HERALD –
17th OCTOBER 1940
– THE WAR NEWS

THE WAR

The past fortnight has been devoid of spectacular incidents on the grand scale.

In the air the R. A. F. has continued its pounding of the sources of German war industry and German occupied ports. Although these attacks are pressed home from low levels our losses of bombers have averaged not more than one in every fifty taking part. After widespread raids on October 12th which included Berlin and Essen it was announced that a heavier type of bomb than ever before is now being used. In Africa also the R. A. F. has made many successful raids on Italian bases and has established a definite ascendency over the Italian air force.

The German air force, feeling its recent heavy losses, has done much less daylight raiding than during the previous month, but has pursued unremittingly the comparatively safe tactics of high altitude night bombing. There can be no immunity from this form of attack, but as, even in England, only a small proportion of the land is not built over so an equal proportion of the bombs explode harmlessly, and military objectives run no more risk than private dwelling houses.

In fact damage to industrial premises has been remarkably small. The London Chamber of Commerce has a membership of over 9,000 firms and up to October 6th only 20 had been compelled to change their addresses owing to damage in air raids, while less than one per cent. of the premises belonging to members of the Manufacturers Trade Association had been hit.

The destruction of private property, especially the poorer class of houses near the London, Liverpool and Cardiff docks, has been serious, but, as the Prime Minister pointed out on October 8th, at the present rate of destruction it would take ten years to destroy half the homes of London.

Air raid casualties for the whole war up to October 7th were 8,500 killed and 13,000 wounded. Living as we do in the safety of North Borneo we must not underestimate the severity of the strain on the civilian population, nor the heroism to which all reports bear witness.

The following is a true story from a private source. A German airman, after parachuting down from his wrecked plane in a country district, surrendered to the first person he met who happened to be an old lady. On the way to the nearest police station the German asked, "Are you people going to give in?" In her astonishment at the suggestion and to her subsequent embarrassment at this lapse from her usual impeccable language, the old lady heard herself ejaculate, "Not bloody likely!" Whereupon the German philosophically remarked, "Well if you don't the German people will".

The slackening of the German daylight attacks has naturally led to a diminution of air losses. The figures are:—

	German planes	British fighters	British pilots saved.
October 1st	4	3	0
„ 2nd	10	4	0
„ 3rd	1	0	0
„ 4th	5	0	0
„ 5th	24	9	5
„ 6th	2	0	0
„ 7th	27	16	10
„ 8th	8	2	0
„ 9th	4	1	1
„ 10th	4	4	1
„ 11th	10	9	6
„ 12th	21	10	8
„ 13th	7	1	1
„ 14th	0	3	0
„ 15th	19	15	0

The danger of invasion is not yet over but grows less day by day. It is known that the Germans have collected sufficient shipping to embark 500,000 troops, but their concentrations have sustained tremendous damage from our bombing attacks.

In the war on land the Italians have spent the last three weeks in consolidating their positions at Sidi Barani and in road making. On October 8th a motor column pushed out beyond Sidi Berani for the first time but was roughly handled by our mechanized units and retired with the loss of ten vehicles. There have also been successful skirmishes on the Sudan and Kenya frontiers.

At the beginning of the month the Mediterranean fleet made another unsuccessful attempt to bring the Italian fleet to battle. In the course of these operations reinforcements were landed at Malta. On October 12th H. M. S. Ajax sighted three Italian destroyers off Sicily and sank two. They were of the 679 A.I ton class. Later on the same day H. M. S. Ajax sighted and engaged a large Italian cruiser and four destroyers. The Italians as usual declined battle but one destroyer was hit and next day was again seen in tow of another destroyer which fled at once. The damaged Italian destroyer was of the latest 1620 ton class and was sunk at leisure. During this period Italian planes attacked our main fleet without causing damage or casualties. Four Italian planes were shot down and two others damaged. H. M. S. Ajax suffered a few casualties but no substantial damage. At the same time the Commander-in-Chief of the Mediterranean fleet reported that British submarines had sunk four Italian supply ships of 5,000, 3,000, 3,000, and 800 tons respectively.

The menace of the U-Boat has not lessened. In the three weeks ending October 6th 202,000 tons of merchant shipping, British, allied and neutral, have been sunk. Against this the Admiralty, breaking its usual silence, has announced the destruction of seven U-Boats and two Italian submarines, and damage to others, in the same period.

It is now known that in the operations at Dakar last month a British battleship and a large cruiser were damaged, while of the Vichy forces two submarines were sunk, two destroyers set on fire, one cruiser damaged and the battleship Richelieu hit several times. On October 10th powerful units of the home fleet assisted the R.A.F. in a terrific bombardment of enemy shipping at Cherbourg. French newspapers state that the German casualties were very heavy.

On October 4th Hitler and Mussolini met at the Brenner pass. Each arrived in an armoured train and fighter planes circled overhead while the conference lasted. The precise subjects of their talks have not been disclosed but the main feature must have been the need to divert the attention of the world from the failure of the Blitzkrieg against England.

On the diplomatic side in Europe the relations of Roumania and Spain to the Axis have been the chief topics of interest. Senor Suner has returned to Madrid after his long consultations in Berlin and Rome, but both the Spanish and Axis papers have preserved a discreet silence about the results of his talks. At the moment the attitude of the Spanish Government is one of unfriendly non-belligerency.

All British subjects have been recommended to leave Roumania following the arrest and ill-treatment of several Englishmen connected with the Roumanian oilfields. It is known that considerable numbers of German troops have arrived in Roumania. Ten divisions are expected and advance units entered Bucharest on October 12th, but the Roumanian Government adheres to the pretence that they are merely "instruc-

270   THE BRITISH NORTH BORNEO HERALD   17th Oct., 1940

tors" for the Roumanian army. The real purpose of the occupation may be only to secure the whole of the Roumanian oil output for Germany or it may be the beginning of an Axis drive to the oilfields of Iraq and Iran. All that can be said with certainty is that Roumania is now enemy occupied territory. The first result of the occupation has been the institution of food rationing—in an agricultural country with a great export of foodstuffs!

It was reported on October 15th that three Roumanian oil wells had caught fire from an unknown cause.

In the Far East there has been considerable tension following the announcement by the Prime Minister that the Burma-Chungking road would be reopened on the expiry of the July agreement on October 18th, but the tension has now lessened. Japan had no moral or legal grounds for requesting that the road should be closed, and Mr. Matsuoka, Foreign Minister of Japan, said that Japan would not "retaliate" for the opening of the road. He has also said that the German-Italian-Japanese pact was designed to spare America from the horrors of war, and that Japan might have to intervene if the war took an unfavourable turn to Germany and Italy. When any speech by a Japanese statesman is considered allowances must be made for the difficulty of translating the exact implications of his language, and also for the situation in which Japan has been placed by her militarists.

The following extract from a Japanese journal of high repute is republished without comment :—

> "Prohibiting the production and sale of luxuries was the first step taken by the (Japanese) Government towards establishing a new order in the daily life of the people. The principal regulations decided by the Home Ministry, the Central Federation of the National Spiritual Mobilization Movement, and other organizations in July and August are the following: (1) All dance halls will be closed permanently on October 31. (2) Gorgeous settings and luxurious costumes on the stage and in motion pictures will be prohibited, along with jazz music and unusually high admission charges. (3) Dining cars in trains will be abolished. (The first step was the abolition of dining cars on the Toh-hoku mainline). (4) The supply of rice to dining rooms attached to Government offices, banks, companies, clubs, assembly halls, and department stores will be temporarily stopped from August 1. (5) From the same day food containing rice will be served at dining rooms and ordinary restaurants only at fixed hours three times a day. (6) Besides banning the use of luxuries, bright coloured clothes, large patterns out of keeping with the age, summer shawls, strangely shaped women's hats, extraordinary high-heeled shoes, eye-shadow, manicures, and conspicuous permanent waves are also prohibited."

Drastic Changes in Living Conditions

Whatever the nuances of Mr. Matsuoka's words may have been they contained the inescapable admission that the pact was a threat to America, and President Roosevelt made a strong speech on October 12th in which he said that America had done with "appeasement" to aggressors in Europe or in Asia. The aggressors, he said, traded on the love of peace among their victims and used "appeasement" as a weapon. He ended his speech by saying "Long live democracy".

On October 14th the U. S. A. Government announced that it would not issue or renew passports for American women or children to Japan, China, Hong Kong, or Indo-China, and that it was sending three liners to evacuate American subjects from Japan and China.

In this country law-abiding people of all races have been welcomed as immigrants, and Japanese enterprise has played a part, although in comparison with British and Chinese a minor part, in the development of the country. According to the most recent statistics the numbers of Japanese subjects resident in N...

OUR GOAL IN THE WAR

FOUR BRITISH IDEALS
LORD GORT ON MISTAKES OF THE PAST

General Lord Gort, V.C., broadcasting on the 4th August during the Sunday evening service recalled that the occasion was the 26th anniversary of the outbreak of the War of 1914-1918. Our goal in the present war, he said, was to ensure that the four characteristics of the soul of Britain—our religious faith, our love of freedom, our sense of tolerance, and our respect for individual rights should survive. Lord Gort said :—

Let us pause on this anniversary to examine some of the reasons which have failed to maintain the peace gained at such immense sacrifice. What has been at fault to bring this new catastrophe upon us? No doubt much that has happened has been beyond our control. We are responsible neither for the ambitions of the leaders of great nations who are today our enemies nor for the failure of their peoples to check their lust for domination. Have we, the British people, been in all respects above reproach? In these last years has our guiding motive been one of patriotism and sacrifice?

Surely you and I are conscious that often selfish and personal considerations have at times taken precedence over the higher ideals of our democratic civilization. In the pursuit of material gain, and possessing, as so many did, a pleasant life, plenty of relaxation, and not too long hours of toil, we were apt to forget that the strength of Britain in the past has been built up on service — service to God, service to our country, and service to our fellow-men. Without this conception of service no great nation can endure. Neglecting our religious obligations and in the pursuit of pleasure, we filled the roads but deserted the churches.

SERVICE IN RETURN

Did we not all too gladly accept the material benefits which came our way without pausing to remember that everything worth having in this world demand some service in return? Is it not possible that reverence — reverence for our country and its traditions, reverence for all that is best in Britain, and, above all, reverence for God, — were lacking in our modern outlook? It is a plain fact that unless a country bases its life on religious faith it cannot endure. And to-day it is evident to every-one of us that we are engaged not solely in a fight for democracy but over and above that in a crusade for the maintenance of those religious principles which we were taught as children by our mothers. The Nazis, too, have a kind of religion, but it is a godless religion based on a material power, and it lacks a moral basis. It is wholly ruthless in conception and sets no store on human life.

Were the Nazi creed to triumph the four characters of the soul of Britain — our religious faith, our love of freedom, our sense of tolerance, and our respect for individual rights would all perish. Our goal is to ensure that these ideals shall survive, and in pursuit of this aim every man and woman in this land is giving his or her very best in the service of Britain.

It has been my fortune to fight alongside two generations of soldiers, and from what I have seen during the past months I know the younger generation are brimful of courage and are ready to

Military Codenames used in World War II

BIRDCAGE
Airborne leaflet drop on Prisoners of War camps announcing Japanese Surrender

FLASH
Codename for attempt on Adolf Hitler's life - March, 1943.

I GO
Japanese codename for Naval counter offensive - April 1943.

KA GO
Japanese reinforcement of Guadalcanal, August 1942, resulting in the battle of the Eastern Solomons.

KATE
NAKAJIMA B5N2 TORPEDO BOMBER
(Code name "Kate" by Allies)

Powered by a 1,000 horsepower Nakajima Sakae II Engine, the "kate" could climb, fully loaded, to 10,000 feet in under eight minutes. With a speed at 10,000 feet at 235 miles per hour, the plane had a ceiling in excess of 25,000 feet and a normal range of 634 miles. Overloaded, range extended to over 1,200 miles. Empty weight 4,830 lbs. Weight when loaded, 8,360 lbs. Wingspan: 50 feet 11 inches. Length: 33 feet 10 inches. armament: One flexible 7.7 mm machine gun in rear cockpit and either one 1,764 lb. torpedo or three 551 lb. bombs.

MAGIC
Operation Magic was the name assigned to the overall U.S. intelligence devoted to breaking Japanese codes.

MALFIST
Planned Allied recapture of Singapore.

MANHATTAN DISTRICT
Cover name for Atomic Bomb project.

MASTIFF
Medical aid to liberated Japanese Prisoners of war camps.

OLYMPIC
Codename for Allied invasion of Kyushu, one of the Japanese home Islands, the opening phase of Operation Downfall, the assault on Japan itself. Olympic was scheduled for November 1945 but was pre-exmpted by Japan's surrender after the dropping of the two Atomic Bombs.

SHO GO
(Operation Victory) Japanese defence plan, summer of 1944. SHO GO embraced several plans, which could be put into effect once the access of Allied advance was made apparent. Plan (1) provide for the defence of the Philippines, Plan (2) the defence of Formosa (Taiwan) and the Ryukyus, Plan (3) the defence of Japan itself, Plan (4) defence of the Kuriles and Hokkaido.

When it was clear the Philippines were the US objective. Plan (1) was put into effect. The Battle of Leyte Gulf ensued.

STARVATION
U.S. Naval operation to mine waters round Japanese home Islands commenced – March 1945.

U GO
Japanese drive on India, from Burma, March, 1944.

VAL
AICHI D3A1 MODEL II DIVE BOMBER
(Code name "Val" by Allies)

A two-seat, carrier-based dive bomber, the "Val" was powered by a 1,000 horsepower Mitsubishi MK8 Kinsei 44 Engine.

The "Val" had a ceiling of 31,200 feet and a speed of 242 miles per hour at 7,500 feet.

Her empty weight was 5,309 lbs. and her full loaded weight 8,041 lbs. The plane had a range of 1,130 miles. Wingspan: 47 feet 1 inch. Length: 33 feet 5 inches.

Armament: Two 7.7 mm forward firing machine guns plus up to 700 lbs. of bombs.

ZEKE
MITSUBISHI A6M2 Zero-sen Fighter
(Code name "Zeke" by Allies)

With a wingspan of 39 feet 4 inches and a length of 29 feet 9 inches, the Zero was powered by a 940 horsepower Nakajima Sakae Engine. Able to climb at nearly 3,000 feet per minute to 20,000 feet, the "Zeke" had a top ceiling of 32,810 feet and a range of 1,160 miles. Top speed was 335 miles per hour. Armament: Two 7.7 mm Mark 3 cannon, and two 132 lbs bombs.

Bibliography

Arnold C. Brackman. The other Nuremberg London WI Collins 1989.

Brigadier Peter Yong. The World Almance of World War II. Bison Books Ltd., London SW5.

Butow, Robert Tojo and the coming of the Princeton, N.J., Princeton University Press, 1961.

Christy Campbell. The World War II Fact Book 1939-1945 Macdonald & Co. (Publishers) Ltd. London

Crow, Carl, ed. Japan's Dream of World Empire: The Tanaka Memorial, Harper & Brothers, 1942.

Eric Robertson. The Japanese File. Heinemann Asia Ltd. Hong Kong, Singapore, Kuala Lumpur (1979)

Gimenez, Pedro M. Under the Shadow of the Kempei. Manila: A. Narvaez, 1946.

Hank Nelson. Prisoners of War. ABC Enterprise – Australian Broadcasting Corporation Sydney NSW 2001.

Maxwell Hall. Kinabalu Guerrillas. Borneo Literature Bureau 1962.

Meyers, Ramon H. and Mark R. Peattie, Eds. The Japanese Colonial Empire, 1895-1945. Princeton University Press, 1982.

Power & Culture: The Japanese American War, 1941-1945. Harvard University Press, 1981.

Sato, Kenryo. Greater East Asia War Memoirs. Tokyo: Tokuma Shoten, 1966.

Scott C.S. Stone. Pearl Harbour. Island Heritage, Honolulu, Hawaii, 1986.

Shillony, Ben-Ami. Politics and Culture in Wartime Japan. Oxford University Press, 1981.

Stan Coben. The East Wind Rain, Pictorial Histories Publishing Company, Missoula, Montana 59801 (1988).

"Still Serving" Vol. 1 December, 1970 Magazine – Chung Nam Printing Co. K.K.

The British North Borneo Herald No. 20 – Vol. LVIII Dated 17th October, 1940. Government Printing Office Sandakan.

Wheeler, Keith. The Fall of Japan, Time Life Books, 1983.

Whelan F.G. Stories from Sabah History, Heinemann Educational Books (Asia) Ltd., Singapore, Hong Kong 1968.

Yefimov D. World War II and Asia's struggle for Independence. New Delhi: Sterling Publishers PVT. LTD.